Fidel Castro

SUTTON POCKET BIOGRAPHIES

Series Editor C.S. Nicholls

Highly readable brief lives of those who have played a significant part in history, and whose contributions still influence contemporary culture.

SUTTON POCKET BIOGRAPHIES

Fidel Castro

CLIVE FOSS

SUTTON PUBLISHING

First published in the United Kingdom in 2000 by
Sutton Publishing Limited · Phoenix Mill
Thrupp · Stroud · Gloucestershire · GL5 2BU

British Library Cataloguing in Publication Data

A catalogue record for this book is available from the British
Library.

ISBN 0-7509-2384-9

Typeset in 13/18 pt Perpetua.
Typesetting and origination by
Sutton Publishing Limited.
Printed in Great Britain by
Cox & Wyman, Reading, Berkshire.

C O N T E N T S

CHRONOLOGY

1926	**13 August.** Fidel Castro born on his father's estate, fifth of nine children
1945–50	Studies law at Havana University
1947	Joins new Ortodoxo party
1948	**April.** Participates in revolution in Bogotá
1949	**12 October.** Marries Mirta Díaz-Balart; divorced in December 1954
1952	**10 March.** Fulgencio Batista seizes power in a coup
1953	**26 July.** Leads attack on Moncada Barracks in Santiago
	October–May 1955. In jail on the Isle of Pines
1955	**July–November 1956.** In exile in Mexico
1956	**2 December.** Lands in Cuba in yacht *Granma*
1957	**17 January.** First rebel victory at La Plata
	17 February. Herbert Matthews interviews Fidel in Sierra Maestra
1958	**May–August.** Unsuccessful army attack on rebels in Sierra Maestra
	31 December. Batista flees Cuba
1959	**2 January.** Fidel's victory speech in Santiago; arrives in Havana on 8 January
	13 February. Becomes prime minister
	April. Visits United States
	8 May. Announces agrarian reform

Chronology

1959	**17 July.** Fidel deposes President Urrutia
1960	**September.** Addresses UN; meets Khrushchev
	13 October. Trade embargo begins
1961	**3 January.** US breaks displomatic relations
	17 April. US-backed Cuban exiles land at Bay of Pigs; swiftly defeated
	1 December. Announces that he is a Marxist-Leninist
1962	**22–8 October.** Missile crisis
1963	**April.** Warmly received in Soviet Union
1967	**9 October.** Che Guevara killed in Bolivia
1968	**March.** Small businesses closed
1970	Ten Million Ton harvest
1971	**November.** Visits Chile as guest of Salvador Allende
1972	**May–June.** Visits Africa, Eastern Europe and Soviet Union
1975	**November.** Cuban troops enter fighting in Angola; stay thirteen years
	December. First Congress of Cuban Communist Party; new constitution announced
1977	**February.** Visits Angola, Somalia and Ethiopia
1979	**August.** Presides over Non-Aligned Nations meeting in Havana
1980	**April.** Mass exodus of dissidents from port of Mariel
1988	**April.** Cuban troops leave Angola
1989	**June.** Trial and execution of General Ochoa, accused of participating in drug traffic
1991	End of Soviet subsidies; beginning of Special Period in Cuba

C h r o n o l o g y

1992   **August.** Riots in Havana; thousands leave on
        makeshift rafts

1993   **July.** Announces economic reforms; legalizes use
        of dollars

1996   **February.** Helms-Burton Act tightens restrictions
        on Cuba

1998   **January.** Pope John Paul II visits Cuba

INTRODUCTION

Fidel Castro is one of the best-known and most enduring of world leaders. Among major rulers, only the Queen of England has been in office longer. Since 1959, Castro has controlled the destiny of Cuba. His instantly recognized beard and army fatigues, symbols of the revolution he led, inspired radicals and revolutionaries who continue to admire him. Others consider him a dictator and a relentless tyrant. Hardly anyone is neutral.

Fidel (as he is universally known) is a man of stupendous abilities and energy. Tall and powerfully built, he is an accomplished sportsman, equally skilled in baseball, basketball, scuba diving and deep-sea fishing. He led a guerrilla war in steep, trackless mountains. He sleeps very little, is constantly on the move, gives innumerable speeches and has written millions of words. He is even a gourmet cook. His prodigious memory and rapid powers of analysis enable him to master virtually any subject and to talk about it for hours. He successfully mobilized world opinion and became an international statesman. Few leaders share his all-round abilities, and few have ever made such a small country the centre of world attention.

Castro has been the subject of hundreds of books, articles and interviews, and yet he remains an enigma. He resolutely guards his private life and presides over a system that tightly controls the flow of information. His long reign over his country makes it difficult to separate Fidel the man from Castro the ruler, and his own life from the history of contemporary Cuba.

This short book attempts to present a basic outline, from his rustic origins, through his studies and political activities in Havana, to his revolutionary leadership and the triumph that allowed him to make fundamental changes, moving Cuba in a new direction, replacing American dominance with communism. In the process, he became a pivotal figure in the Cold War, and a leader of the Third World. Finally, he has managed to keep his country and its system going despite unparalleled economic catastrophes.

I have tried to tell Fidel's story more than Cuba's but the two are inextricably intertwined. Since he is still in power, no final judgement is possible. History may view him as a revolutionary hero who spread the idea of liberation through the world or as an ossified despot who has transformed one of the richest countries of Latin America into one of the poorest. Most likely, he combines the elements of both.

Mina Marefat read the manuscript with intricate care, and Ken Brosiner provided detailed criticisms; both saved it from many errors and infelicities. William MacDonald and Ubaldo Huerta made many helpful suggestions. In Havana, Silvia Orta's tireless efforts opened doors; Nelida Mesa and a group of Moncada veterans brought the revolution to life; and Naty Revuelta generously contributed a vivid personal perspective. My thanks to them all, and to Cuba itself whose places and people inspired the pages that follow.

GROWING UP CUBAN, 1926–45

Fidel Castro, who brought communism to Cuba, was the son of a very rich man. The house where he was born stands in lush rolling country about ten miles from the sea, in the eastern part of the island. This massive wooden structure was untypically built on piles so the cattle could stay at ground level, while the family occupied the upper floors. Broad verandas, big salons and several bedrooms made it airy and comfortable. A separate wing served for conducting business and paying the workers, for this was the centre of an active estate. Beside the mansion were a large store, butcher's shop, post office and hotel, along the road that led from the coast to Santiago, metropolis of Cuba's Oriente province. The complex also included a small schoolhouse and shacks for the immigrant workers, while a pit for cockfights provided entertainment.

All this was the work of Angel Castro, who left the impoverished north-west of Spain to fight with the Spanish army against the Cuban Revolution in 1898. He stayed on in Cuba, first peddling lemonade, then working on the railroad. He eventually bought a lumber mill and leased land from the powerful American United Fruit Company. He ended up controlling a vast tract of 25,000 acres, much of it planted in sugar processed by a nearby American mill. Angel Castro became one of the greatest landowners in Oriente, the roughest part of Cuba, but also the area most subject to American influence.

The war that Angel had joined led to Cuban independence, but not in a form the rebels had envisioned. After bitter fighting had gone on for three years, the United States intervened, defeated the Spaniards, and liberated the country. For Americans, the Spanish–American War was a heroic action, freeing Spain's last colony in the New World. Many Cubans, though, thought the revolution had been snatched from their hands, with a new master replacing the old. After four years of US military occupation Cuba finally gained independence in 1902, but with an important qualification. The Platt Amendment allowed the Americans to intervene as necessary to ensure stability. They intervened militarily and politically well into the 1920s. As a result, Cuban nationalism became strongly anti-American. Its great hero and theoretician, José Martí, who was killed early in the war, had already voiced his suspicions of his powerful neighbour's intentions.

A vast influx of American investment followed the war, whose ferocity and devastation had ruined the Cuban land-owning aristocracy. American companies took over the railways, public utilities and Cuba's greatest industry, sugar. A tropical country with few natural resources, Cuba was ideally suited for producing sugar, which was grown on huge estates and demanded heavy investment in mills and distribution systems. Money and industrial products naturally came from the United States, only 90 miles away. Oriente province, in particular, was dominated by the mills and model American-style towns of one company, United Fruit, from which Angel Castro derived most of his wealth.

Angel married a schoolteacher who bore him two children, Pedro Emilio and Lidia, but his attention soon shifted to a young housemaid, Lina Ruz, who produced seven more: Angela, Ramón, Fidel, Raúl,

Juana, Emma and Agustina. Some time after the birth of the first three, Angel married Lina.

Fidel Castro was born at Birán on 13 August 1926 and named after an influential local politician. Despite the family's wealth, he grew up in a rustic and unsophisticated atmosphere. Angel Castro, a frugal and tough, even ferocious, master, was no aristocrat. The family was notoriously chaotic and quarrelsome; chickens roosted everywhere in the house, except in Angel's office. Yet his parents and sisters always gave Fidel important moral and financial support.

From his earliest years, Fidel loved sport and the country, and played happily with the children of his father's Haitian labourers. The rough manners and language he learned sometimes shocked his mother, but he remained her favourite child. His relations with his father were much more difficult. He learned his first lessons in the one-room school on the family property, where he was an unruly child who hated authority of any kind. As a result, the six-year-old Fidel was sent off to the Catholic La Salle school in Santiago. For that, he was baptised and his parents married. In Santiago, he lived with his godfather, the Haitian consul, whom he claimed didn't feed him enough. He made so much trouble that he was enrolled as a boarder, which improved his mood but not his disposition. He always pushed to be first in everything and got into fights with his classmates and teachers. Fidel longed for the holidays when he could return to the country to ride, swim and climb. After he tried to lead a student strike he and his brothers, considered the worst bullies in the school, were brought home. Fidel refused to stay, threatening to burn down the house, until his parents relented and let him return to school.

At the age of nine, Fidel entered the Dolores school in Santiago, where he began the Jesuit education that was to influence him deeply. He liked history (especially military history), geography, and stories of famous men like the Cuban patriot Martí. But his favourite activity was sport, where his outstanding skills gained the respect of his fellow students, who had looked down on him as a bumpkin. In these years, he began to explore the nearby Sierra Maestra mountains. The Jesuits taught him a spartan lifestyle, but not the rebelliousness that made him try to organize a strike among his father's workers when he was thirteen. By now he was growing aware of the outside world. When Franklin

Roosevelt was re-elected in 1940, the fourteen-year-old Fidel wrote him a letter of congratulation, asking for 'a ten dollars bill green American' and claiming to be twelve. Although the president didn't answer directly, the response Fidel received from the State Department was proudly posted on the school's noticeboard.

In September 1941 Fidel entered a new world in Havana, the vibrant, sensual and sophisticated capital. He enrolled in the elite Belén school, the best in the country. Its Jesuit masters taught seriously and enforced strict discipline; the boys wore uniforms and attended mass. Many of them came from Franco's Spain and advocated the superiority of Spanish culture. Fidel delved into the works of the Spanish fascists as well as Mussolini and Hitler; ideas of liberal democracy had little influence here. The teenage Fidel concentrated only on the subjects he liked (Spanish, history, geography and agriculture) and devoted most of his effort to sport. He became head of the hiking club, and invariably took the lead in mountain climbing. When the coach of the basketball team rejected him, he threw himself into practice, even asking the padre to install a light so he could continue after hours. His work paid off: he not only joined the team, but became its captain in his senior year.

Fidel won his first great distinction at the age of eighteen, when he was named Cuba's outstanding collegiate athlete. His prowess in sport once again overcame the disdain that his aristocratic classmates felt for this rough rustic brawler. Nevertheless, Fidel never lost the resentment of the upper classes that his school experience generated. Love of sport meant that he often neglected his studies, but his incredible memory saved him. When his schoolmates asked him what was on a given page of the sociology text, he would respond by quoting all of it from memory. In his last year, he was excluded from the exams in French and logic because he hadn't attended the classes. He persuaded the teacher to let him take the exams as long as he succeeded in getting 100 per cent in French; he did. Determination, concentrated hard work, memory and sport became the foundation of his career.

Fidel's all-round abilities earned him special recognition. When he graduated in 1945 the head of the school prophetically wrote in his yearbook: 'He has known how to win the admiration and affection of all. He will make law his career and we do not doubt that he will fill with brilliant pages the book of his life'.[1]

While Fidel was growing up, Cuba was passing through a period of turmoil. He was born during the presidency of Gerardo Machado who entered office as a reformer and builder, but soon became power-hungry and corrupt. In a country that had no tradition of democracy, politics was seen as the prime route to riches: high offices were bitterly contested and vast sums were stolen. After his fraudulent re-election in 1928, Machado was faced with economic disaster brought by the Great Depression. He responded with force. In November 1930 he suspended the constitution, censored the press, and despatched secret police and death squads against those who dared to oppose him. Cubans, who had never known dictatorship, resisted, led by students and communists. They had little success until F.D. Roosevelt came to power in Washington. He sent a special emissary who negotiated with the opposition and forced Machado to leave the country in August 1933. An American-backed liberal regime took over. The country was in chaos; bloody reprisals against Machado's followers, communism spreading among the sugar workers, and resentment of a government installed by foreigners provoked a coup. Sgt Fulgencio Batista allied with the students to establish a radical professor, Ramón Grau San Martín, in power. The hundred days of this government were a heroic time for the students and radicals, but American opposition doomed it.

Finally, in January 1934, Batista, with the approval of Washington, overthrew the government, crushed all opposition and re-established stability. Batista was another native of Oriente province, of very humble background. A mulatto in a society that practised racial discrimination, he had drifted through a series of jobs (apparently at one point working for Angel Castro) until he joined the army, where he served as a stenographer. A persuasive speaker, he became the leader of the sergeants and corporals who overthrew first their officers, then the government. His reward was cancellation of the hated Platt Amendment and negotiation of a favourable trade treaty that guaranteed a market for Cuban sugar in the United States. Batista chose the presidents who restored prosperity and produced the liberal Constitution of 1940. This incorporated a range of social benefits and limited the president to one term, but allowed him to suspend civil rights for forty-five days at a time in an emergency. The same year, in the first reasonably honest election since 1912, Batista became president. He followed progressive policies, in close alliance with the United States. In 1944, though, his chosen candidate was surprisingly beaten by Grau San Martín, the radical of 1933. Real changes seemed imminent.

Fidel went home for the summer of 1945, persuaded his father to buy him a new Ford, and returned to Havana, where he and his sisters moved into an apartment near the university. He enrolled in the faculty of law.

THE RISING
POLITICIAN,
1945–52

L earning was not the only activity at the
university, whose elegant neoclassical buildings
crown a hill in the centre of Havana. Since 1934 the
university had been a special area where the police
could not enter. In theory it was run by the
democratically elected heads of the student unions
who chose their own president. In practice, rival
bands of professional gangsters, for whom it was the
ideal refuge, controlled the campus. Some were
students, others, often in their thirties, had only the
loosest connection with studies. They flourished
under the regime of Grau, who exchanged radicalism
for corruption. Huge sums looted from government
contracts and offices supported organized thugs,
'students' who were a valuable counterweight to an

army which still supported Batista. Gangs harassed students and professors, monopolized the sale of textbooks and exam papers and fixed exam marks. The two most important were the Social Revolutionary Movement (MSR) and the Insurrectional Revolutionary Union (UIR), whose armed fighters decided student elections. Rather than suppressing the gangs, Grau gave their leaders senior posts in the police, and provided jobs to many of their followers. Gangsters and politicians were closely allied in a system that left little room for traditional learning.

In October 1945 Fidel Castro entered a world where his excellent education and distinction in sport counted for little. The university had no athletics and its formal education was perfunctory. Poorly paid professors did as little work as possible and students needed only to memorize material for the final exams (if they hadn't already bought the papers). An ambitious graduate of Cuba's best school, studying law – the normal route to wealth and power – would naturally turn to student politics. In his first few months there, Fidel won election as a law school delegate to the Student Union, but never rose higher. His intense determination to be first in everything made him impossible to work with; the communists would have nothing to do with him because he couldn't be controlled; and the gangs were the only ones who counted. In December 1946, during his second year, Fidel decided to enter the power structure: he reputedly shot a fellow-student in order to win the favour of the MSR leader. Yet he was no mere gunslinger, for in November he had made his debut as a public speaker at a meeting where he denounced the greed and corruption of the government, as well as the gangs. This gained him his first notice in the newspaper; he was not yet twenty-one. Far more astute than most of his classmates, Fidel adopted violence and politics at the same time.

When President Grau made it clear that his crony Prío Socarrás would be his successor, Eddie Chibás, a rich congressman and student leader of the 1930s, whose radio broadcasts incessantly denounced corruption, broke away and formed a new party. Fidel was the only student leader to attend the first meeting of the so-called Ortodoxos on 15 May 1947. He threw himself into the movement, leading the revolutionary Radical Orthodox Action group and recruiting youth, especially from Oriente province. The same month he gave his first formal speech,

addressing the student delegates on the anniversary
of the university charter. His powerful attack on false
leaders and the gangs earned enthusiastic applause
and got his picture in the newspapers. It also brought
the enmity of the MSR and its allies in government,
who sent Fidel a threatening message. He walked on
the beach and reflected. Determined not to be
intimidated, he returned to the university armed.
Fear never stopped him.

By now, Fidel had adopted a distinctive lifestyle.
He made no pretence of studying, but threw himself
into politics. His social life consisted entirely of
political meetings or of efforts to persuade people to
join him. When he tried to make deals, he treated
each individual as his intimate friend, so much so that
his way of speaking became a joke. But Fidel did not
tolerate jokes at his expense. Nor did he drink or
dance (unheard of in a Cuban), or chase girls. In fact,
in his uniform of wool suit and tie, he was extremely
shy with women. His energies were devoted to his
faction, for whom he edited a mimeographed bulletin
and constantly recruited members.

In the summer of 1947 Castro joined his first
foreign adventure. The MSR and a group of
Dominican exiles organized an expedition against the

dictator Rafael Trujillo. Despite his membership of the rival UIR gang, Fidel was accepted and received his first military training. Before the group could move, however, the United States put pressure on Grau, who sent a gunboat to stop the attack. Meanwhile, the head of the UIR was killed in a gunfight with the MSR, leaving Fidel exposed to his rivals. Consequently, as the men were being brought back to the capital, he jumped ship and swam eight miles across shark-infested waters to take refuge at Birán, where he lay low for a short time. The aborted expedition gave Fidel a first taste for military uniforms, weapons and adventure.

He was soon back in Havana, leading demonstrations against the notorious minister of education, who eventually left for Miami with $20 million in his suitcase. Fidel developed his skills as speaker and leader as he continued to denounce government corruption. He worked with Chibás (though the two were not on especially close terms), who took the high road, leaving Fidel to organize street demonstrations. Frequent attention from the press was making him the best-known opposition leader after Chibás himself. But at the same time, he ran ever greater risks from the MSR, especially after he was accused of participating in the murder of one of its leaders. The capital was becoming so dangerous that Fidel welcomed an opportunity to leave the country.

In March 1948 Argentina's dictator Juan Perón, ever looking for ways to thwart the Yankees, organized a congress of radical students in Bogotá to coincide with the first meeting of the Organization of American States. Argentine money financed a group of Cuban students, which Fidel willingly joined. They arrived in the Colombian capital on 7 April, planning to meet the charismatic labour leader Eliazar Gaitán. Just before their appointment though, Gaitán, a genuine popular hero and hope of the left, was assassinated, and the city broke into violent revolt. Mobs stormed and looted the capital. Fidel happily joined them, riding in a jeep and seizing weapons from the police. The revolt soon collapsed, but Fidel gained invaluable experience and learned that a popular revolution could not succeed without a leader. He became convinced that he could be such a leader. The Cuban students were accused of communism, but there is no evidence that Fidel then shared that doctrine or any other.

He returned home in time for the presidential election on 1 June which Prío Socarrás, backed by the unions and massive bribes, easily won. No one dreamed that these would be Cuba's last free elections. A few days later a police sergeant who was shot named Fidel as his assailant, but no evidence was ever produced. Violence continued through the autumn and into the new year, with Fidel joining in demonstrations and clashing with the police. However, his life soon took an uncharacteristic turn.

On 12 October 1948, Fidel married the only girl he had courted, Mirta Díaz-Balart, the sister of a close friend and daughter of a rich politician from Oriente who was Batista's lawyer and later interior minister. The wedding took place in the church at Banes, near Birán. Mirta, like most of Fidel's later loves, was blonde, elegant and socially well connected. Her parents were less delighted than Fidel's, but both collaborated to give a lavish wedding. Fulgencio Batista even gave the happy couple $1,000. They spent their honeymoon in New York, where Fidel briefly studied English (he could eventually speak it fluently but idiosyncratically), then returned to Havana, supported by an allowance from old Angel. The marriage soon turned sour as Fidel could not turn his attention away from politics, was constantly away at meetings and demonstrations, and earned no money.

When she became pregnant, Mirta's life became harder for she never knew whether the rent would be paid or basic needs provided. Their son, Fidelito, was born on 1 September 1949.

Fidel's fame and notoriety grew. When American sailors desecrated the statue of Cuba's hero José Martí, Fidel conspicuously formed the honour guard around it. His voice was heard on the radio and he constantly visited poor districts and protested against racism. But his attacks on the government, particularly a well-reported speech in November 1949 against the pact between politicians and the gangs, again forced him into hiding. He went back to New York for a few months. On his return, he finally crammed for the law school exams. His stupendous memory and capacity for concentrated effort enabled him to do two years' work in six months, and to graduate in September 1950.

The new lawyer, with his excellent connections, could have established a lucrative practice, but chose instead to take a tiny office in Old Havana and devote his efforts to the poor, students and workers. He gained more popularity than income, but he never had any interest in money. Unfortunately he had a wife, who was not pleased to find the furniture repossessed for non-payment, or to have to borrow money from friends to buy milk for the child. Fidel had other cares.

On 5 August 1950, in a supremely dramatic gesture, Eddie Chibás shot himself during his radio programme because he could not produce the evidence that he had promised against the education minister. Fidel rushed to his bedside, kept vigil there, then presided over the funeral. He was still too young to lead the party, but for many he inherited Chibás' mantle as defender of the people against corruption. This was the first of several instances of leaders disappearing from the scene, easing Fidel's path to power. More active than ever in politics, he explored every avenue, even meeting with Batista, with whom he allegedly discussed a military coup. By now, he had valuable support in his brother Raúl, who was at university studying sociology and drawing ever closer to the communists.

A huge headline, I ACCUSE, announced Fidel's detailed exposé of President Prío's corruption on 28 January 1952. This was a real sensation, pushing the rising politician further into the limelight. He now threw his ferocious energies into the campaign for Congress in the 1952 elections. Using modern but unparalleled techniques he travelled all over Havana province, sometimes giving four speeches in an afternoon, sent out 100,000 personal letters (he used a stencil, something new in Cuba), and appeared on the radio every day. His continuing exposure of the government and the gangs assured him support in the poor districts of Havana. By now he was too famous for the gangs to try to assassinate him.

Everything indicated that the 25-year-old Fidel Castro would join the next government and become leader of a radical faction. In fact, as he later revealed, he planned to exploit constitutional means to make major changes. Once elected, he would break party discipline and mobilize the population for a revolutionary programme to smash the existing power structure and promote drastic social change. Neither he nor anyone else, though, had counted on Batista who, realizing that he had no chance in the coming elections, followed a simpler course. On 10 March 1952 he took over the main army base, Camp Columbia on the outskirts of Havana. President Prío fled the country. Politics came to a sudden end.

THREE

THE REBEL,
1952–6

Cuba's public shared Batista's disgust with corruption; few missed the politicians or resisted the military. An announced general strike fizzled out and student riots attracted no support. Batista, the champion of law and order, announced that he would hold power only until elections in 1953. He made himself provisional president, dissolved Congress, and ruled by decree; military men took over the government. Many politicians fled into exile, while the new regime's revelations of corruption undermined the position of the rest. By May Batista felt strong enough to restore civil rights and look forward to a period of peaceful prosperity. He was a dictator who promised democracy.

Fidel Castro went into hiding on the news of the coup, but soon emerged, determined to overthrow the dictatorship. The suppression of politics convinced him that armed struggle was the only real route to change; but he also used the law. A fortnight after the coup, the lawyer Fidel filed a brief against Batista, charging that his coup was illegal according to the constitution. He knew such attacks could not succeed, but they guaranteed publicity. In more practical terms, Castro began to build support for a revolution.

On May Day 1952 a small group of militants met at the Colon cemetery to celebrate the memory of an assassinated student leader. Among them were a young accountant, Abel Santamaría, and his sister Haydée, both Ortodoxos, members of a group that met regularly to discuss politics and the writings of José Martí. In them, Fidel found the core for a revolutionary organization, and the group found the leader it needed. Fidel introduced strict physical and ideological discipline, organized a cell structure so that the group would survive if individuals were captured or betrayed, established regular meetings and produced a publication called *The Accuser*. The clandestine organization, based in Abel's apartment, slowly began to spread, attracting followers from the many parts of Cuba that Fidel visited. By the end of 1952 it had 150 widely scattered cells and claimed 1,200 members.

Many others opposed Batista. Politicians, notably ex-president Prío who planned to use his stolen wealth to finance an invasion, agitated from exile, while the National Revolutionary Movement of middle-class liberals hoped for military support. This organization attracted many young militants, but Castro refused to join: he had no desire to cooperate with the army, or to work for a group he didn't lead. Batista also faced hostility from the upper classes who longed for democracy or despised him as a mulatto.

Batista allowed a free press and tolerated protest meetings. On 27 November Fidel attended the annual commemoration of the medical students shot by the Spanish. So did Naty Revuelta, a gorgeous green-eyed blonde, who had been the toast of aristocratic Havana. Rich and well-connected, she instantly fell for Fidel and became his devoted follower, although she was married to a respectable doctor. Student riots continued, but Fidel only joined them on Martí's centenary in January 1953 when he led 500 of his followers in a spectacular torchlight parade.

Since Fidel's movement aimed at armed revolution, its members had regular target practice and a commando course. Most of them were workers and Ortodoxos, with few students and no communists. They were short of money and guns. Members willingly sacrificed their businesses or possessions, and sympathizers contributed money (Naty sold her jewels), but weapons for a revolution would have to be seized from an army base. Since Camp Columbia in Havana was powerfully defended, the Moncada barracks in Santiago seemed to offer better possibilities, especially during the festival of St James in July, when the guard would be small and distracted.

Planning was systematic and highly secret. Weapons, mostly sport and hunting guns, were bought and hidden in Naty's house. Military training continued, constantly changing sites, and a farmhouse was rented at Siboney outside Santiago as the base for the attack. Abel Santamaría went to prepare it in June, while Naty, Haydée and the other women sewed Cuban army uniforms. Fidel's plan made some sense. He would capture the barracks, seize the weapons, distribute them to the population of the ever-rebellious Oriente province and proclaim the revolution from a liberated territory. Another detachment would simultaneously capture the fort at

Bayamo on the Central Highway to prevent reinforcements from arriving. If all failed, they could retreat to the nearby impenetrable mountains of the Sierra Maestra. Fidel brought together a force of 163 men and 2 women, who had no idea what was in store. Even Raúl, who had spent June at a Russian-sponsored Youth and Student Festival, only learned at the last minute.

On 24 July Fidel and his band left Havana in small groups, by train, bus and car. His last stop was at Naty's, where he left the text of the manifesto to be broadcast when the expedition succeeded. The document was hardly revolutionary, promising the restoration of democracy and the Constitution in the context of nationalism and social justice. After stopping at Bayamo to organize the attack there, Fidel assembled 135 followers at Siboney, and revealed his goal: to capture the fortress at dawn the next day, 26 July. Only a tiny handful backed down.

Fidel drove into town as the sun was rising and the locals were returning from their revels. Two small bands, led by Abel Santamaría and Raúl, successfully occupied the Civil Hospital and Palace of Justice near the barracks, but part of the convoy took a wrong turn and never found the scene of action. When the driver of the first car got the drowsy guard to open the gate by telling him that the General was arriving, the rebels penetrated the defences and secured the surrender of fifty soldiers. At this point, though, a patrol unexpectedly appeared, the alarm sounded and a firefight began. Fidel immediately realized he had no chance and ordered a retreat. He and a few men reached the hills, while others scattered through the city. The infuriated army commander ordered ten attackers killed for every dead soldier. As a result, more than fifty were caught and murdered. The worst scene took place in the hospital, where Haydée Santamaría was presented with the torn-out eye of her brother. Her refusal to admit anything was a vignette of heroism in a heroic day.

A few days later government troops caught up with Fidel. With the luck that accompanied him all his life, his captors delivered him to the police rather than the army. This action saved his life, though not his freedom. The remnants of his men were put on trial in September; Fidel's defence of them together with the gruesome stories they told gained so much sympathy that most were acquitted, but 29, including the leaders and the 2 women, were sentenced to prison. Fidel by now was such a hero that the government feared the publicity of an open trial. On 16 October he was tried separately in a hospital room.

Fidel the lawyer conducted his own defence, a five-hour indictment of the regime, full of classical and legal learning and given without notes. He enumerated Batista's crimes, claimed that his revolt against an illegal regime was itself legal, and announced a revolutionary programme. Had he succeeded, he planned to restore the Constitution of 1940, reform the judiciary, redistribute land to smallholders, confiscate ill-gotten gains, nationalize the Trusts, reduce rents, build housing and promote industrialization. Fidel remained faithful to this coherent programme, socialist rather than communist, when he eventually came to power. But few in 1953 imagined that day would ever come, since he had been condemned to fifteen years. He expected the sentence, but looked beyond it. His speech concluded: 'I do not fear prison, just as I do not fear the fury of the miserable tyrant who snatched the life from seventy of my brothers. Sentence me; it doesn't matter; history will absolve me.'[1] These words long resounded through Cuba.

Fidel and his men spent their terms in the hospital wing of Machado's model prison in the Isle of Pines, where they were treated as political prisoners. They could receive mail and occasional visitors and cook their own food. Fidel exploited his enforced idleness to educate his men and himself. He set up a regular school, with classes five hours a day, using books sent in by sympathizers. For the only time in his adult life, Fidel had leisure for extensive reading. He educated himself in his favourite subjects, including Marxism, which he now came to understand and appreciate, and enjoyed books about the Soviet Union. He discussed his readings in regular and often passionate correspondence with Naty. His letters to his wife Mirta, who came to visit, were more perfunctory. On one occasion he saved time by sending the same letter to both; unfortunately (or deliberately) the censor switched the letters and the faithful Mirta learned the truth.

Prison school and relative comfort came to a sudden end when Batista visited the prison on 12 February 1954. To his fury, the Moncada rebels greeted him with their revolutionary hymn. This brought solitary confinement for Fidel. Yet he could still write letters and smuggle out secret messages in cigars, cigarette boxes and invisible ink between the lines of normal letters. By these means, his speech, *History Will Absolve Me*[1] (which Fidel reconstructed from memory), reached the outside world. The two women who had participated in the attack, Haydée and Melba Hernández, were released in February. They became his best agents for keeping the movement alive. In June an interview with the popular magazine *Bohemia* (which had already proclaimed him one of the twelve outstanding figures of 1953) ensured that he remained Cuba's most famous political prisoner. The only sour note came in July when he learned that his wife had lost her job in the Interior Ministry. This was essentially a post without duties created by her brother to keep her in funds, but for Fidel, who knew nothing of it, it was pure treason to be working for the government that had imprisoned him. Divorce followed in December.

Batista brought prosperity, at least to the rich. Skyscrapers started to rise and Havana could boast more Cadillacs per capita than any city in the world. Gambling (run by the US Mafia), prostitution and other attractions brought masses of tourists who rarely noticed the growing rings of slums around the cities. A sense of security allowed the president to yield to the appeals of the prisoners' mothers and declare a general amnesty. On 15 May 1955 Fidel was released in a flood of publicity; he told reporters that he believed in democracy and the Ortodoxos. Yet he was the head of something new, which he named the 26 July Movement after the date of the Moncada attack.

Back in Havana, Fidel resumed his old activities, writing, speaking and broadcasting against the dictatorship in an atmosphere of growing violence. Opposition was growing as the economic position of the poor declined; Batista responded with repression that gradually closed in on Fidel. Magazines that published him were closed, many of his supporters were arrested. He saw that his only option was exile, to be followed by armed revolt. Yet he had consolation: Naty met him on his arrival in Havana and their affair flourished; in June she conceived Fidel's daughter Alina.

On 7 July Fidel flew to Mexican exile; Raúl had preceded him. Living in cheap hotels and boarding houses, he met Cuban dissidents and Mexican leftists, never losing sight of his goal of returning to Cuba to lead the revolution. His most fateful meeting came within a fortnight when Raúl introduced him to an

Argentine doctor, Ernesto 'Che' Guevara. Slightly younger than Fidel, he had left Buenos Aires in 1953 on a year-long journey to struggle against American imperialism. Che, an ideologue and a Marxist, was instantly attracted to Fidel who became the inspiration for the rest of his life. He provided intellectual depth for the practical 26 July Movement. Che was content to listen and persuade, never to argue with Fidel, who had no tolerance for open disagreement. The two became inseparable comrades.

Fidel made sure that he was not forgotten at home. When the Ortodoxos held their congress in August, he sent a manifesto calling for immediate elections without Batista and advocating the programme he had proclaimed. This gained him support among the rank and file who started to form a nucleus for his movement in Cuba. Their leaders included Frank País, an intense young schoolteacher, and Celia Sánchez, daughter of a radical physician, both from Oriente. Fidel had already decided on guerrilla warfare, and planned a landing on the coast near the Sierra Maestra mountains. Frank and Celia obtained the appropriate maps and organized the movement at home, while Fidel devoted himself to raising money.

Life in Mexico was expensive because of the bribes the Cubans needed to pay to stay ahead of the law. Since the Cuban community in the United States offered the best hope for raising money, Fidel left for Miami on 10 October. His speeches, which attracted enthusiastic audiences, included an announcement in New York that Cuba would be free or his men would be martyrs before the end of 1956. He had committed himself to a specific deadline.

Meanwhile, events were moving ahead in Cuba. Late in 1955, the charismatic student leader José Antonio Echeverría organized the Revolutionary Directorate which began a campaign of urban sabotage and armed resistance. Although the workers did not join him, they began a series of strikes which shook the government far more than the sporadic violence of the students. Fidel controlled none of this.

After returning to Mexico Fidel found a suitable instructor for the recruits who started coming in from Cuba. He persuaded General Alberto Bayo, a guerrilla veteran of the Spanish civil war, to devote himself to training the Cubans. The men came under full military discipline, with conspiratorial secrecy, constant exercise, mountain climbing and training with weapons. They got up at 5 a.m., walked several miles to ever-changing meeting places and were allowed little contact with each other; even the leaders, if they wanted to go out on dates, had to go in pairs. Money from Cuba and the United States enabled the movement to acquire a farmhouse outside Mexico City, where their activities could escape notice. Their training filled most of 1956.

Money remained a constant problem, especially after Fidel's arrest in June for conspiracy. He was denounced in the papers as a communist, and only released after the former president Lázaro Cárdenas intervened. He faced an order to leave within two weeks, which meant more bribes. During Fidel's stay in prison, the Cuban cultural attaché, Teresa Casuso, visited Fidel. She soon became his greatest local backer, allowing her house to be used for meetings and storing weapons, but did not attract Fidel's affection. That went to a beautiful eighteen-year-old, Isabel Custodio, for whom Fidel even started to adopt uncharacteristic neatness. Unfortunately, she preferred romance to politics and married someone else. Typically, Fidel's conversation dealt with politics and his attraction to women was usually limited to their interest in his goals.

Fidel also had his women and children in Cuba. He remained in touch with Naty and reportedly offered to marry her after the birth of their daughter, but she stayed in Havana. Relations with Mirta were less friendly since both wanted custody of their son Fidelito, who came to Mexico for a fortnight's visit in September. When Fidel tried to keep the child, Mirta had to call on the Mexican and Cuban authorities to get him back. She became a sad drifter, sometimes working in a Florida restaurant, but soon remarried. Fidel had yet another son, Jorge Angel, by a woman named Amparo, whom he had met during a brief trip to Oriente. Although the women often faded from his life, he never forgot his children.

One man had all the money the rebels needed, and was willing to use it to support revolution – Fidel's former nemesis, ex-president Prío. Ignoring the past, Fidel met him in Texas in September through the intermediary of Teresa Casuso, and received $50,000 in cash. His money problems were over, but not his political ones. In August, Echeverría had come to Mexico to make a deal with Fidel. He refused to subordinate his movement to Fidel's, but did sign an agreement which established formal co-operation between the two.

Plans for the armed landing were now advanced. Despite warnings that his support network was not ready, Fidel was determined to reach Cuba in 1956. With Prío's money he bought weapons and an old wooden 56-foot yacht, named *Granma* by its American owner after his grandmother. The Mexicans forced his hand. On 21 November they arrested Teresa Casuso and other Cubans, confiscated stores of weapons and gave Fidel seventy-two hours to leave the country. He brought his men to the coast, cheered them with the false news that 50,000 armed rebels were waiting for them, and embarked from the port of Tuxpan on the 25th.

Fidel had planned a five-day trip to coincide with an uprising in Santiago led by Frank País. He hadn't counted on the slow progress of the overloaded boat, filled with eighty-two men, weapons, ammunition and supplies, or on bad weather, mechanical problems and seasickness. As it turned out, the expedition missed the uprising (when País actually managed to occupy key points in the city and burn the police station) and the planned rendezvous with Celia Sánchez and Crescencio Pérez, the bandit chief of the Sierra Maestra. Instead, the boat stuck on mud and the occupants had to wade ashore through waist-deep water and a painful mangrove swamp. Finally, on 2 December 1956, Fidel kept his promise. Like José Martí in 1895, he had returned to liberate Cuba.

FOUR

THE HERO,
1956—8

I̲n̲ Cuban legend, Fidel with his twelve men
brought freedom and salvation. If the parallels
with Jesus Christ were exaggerated, the reality was
not altogether different. Two years and one month
after his landing, Fidel ruled Cuba. His tiny band won
victory, not so much through fighting as effective
propaganda, unremitting sabotage in the cities, the
disappearance of rivals, Batista's growing
unpopularity, and crucial decisions in Washington.

The beginning was bad: three days after the
landing, Fidel's force was ambushed and virtually
destroyed. The sixteen survivors scattered in the hills
and only gradually reunited during December. But
Fidel's confidence never wavered. When Raúl brought
two rifles to add to his five, Fidel cried 'Now, yes, we
have won the war'.[1] In fact, though, they were
refugees in the wild Sierra Maestra whose steep and

broken ridges stretch a hundred miles along the south coast of Cuba. They had entered a land of the dispossessed and discontented who lived by growing coffee or burning charcoal. Many of them were squatters in an eternal conflict with the stewards of the great estates that ringed the mountain. Fidel's greatest hope lay in these peasants, who sheltered his men, and especially in their leaders like Crescencio Pérez, who reputedly controlled thousands.

The new year found a prosperous Cuba filled with tourists, but suffering from urban sabotage. Most of its people believed the official announcement that Fidel Castro had been killed; few even heard of his first victory, on 17 January 1957. That dawn, with twenty-eight men, Fidel attacked the tiny garrison at La Plata on the coast. His men captured and burned the barracks, carrying off weapons, ammunition and food, with no losses of their own. It was the first rebel victory, a great psychological milestone that showed they could strike at will. It was almost their last, for during the next weeks a traitor revealed their positions to Batista's air force. He even managed to sleep under Fidel's blanket one night but didn't have the nerve to kill him; he was soon caught and executed. Fidel had made his laws: insubordination, desertion and defeatism would be punished with death.

As Che Guevara later remarked, 'The presence of a foreign journalist, preferably American, was more important for us than military victory'.[2] The Rebel Army's victories were always on a small scale; it was the American press that built Fidel's reputation. In a sense, his greatest success in the Sierra came on 17 February, when a veteran *New York Times* reporter, Herbert Matthews, reached the rebel camp. Fidel gave an extensive interview and showed off his men with great theatrical success. Matthews never guessed that there were only eighteen of them, since Raúl paraded by several times with the same men and a sentry rushed in breathlessly to announce a message from a non-existent second column.

Matthews returned to write a series of articles that transformed the obscure rebel into a universal hero. The first, on the front page of the *New York Times* on 24 February, began, 'Fidel Castro, the rebel leader of Cuba's youth, is alive and fighting hard and successfully', and continued in a romantic vein describing Fidel and his numerous men, the failures of the army to defeat them, their extensive support among the people, and their doctrine: Fidel was a nationalist, who believed in democracy and opposed communism. When the articles appeared in Cuba a week later (by coincidence, censorship had just been lifted) they caused a sensation. They also brought ridicule on the government which claimed that Fidel had been killed. The cartoon the conservative American *National Review* published in 1960 showing Fidel standing over Cuba with the caption 'I got my job through the *New York Times*' was not altogether facetious.[3] The *Times* did not have the field to itself for long. In April, the American TV network CBS sent a crew that filmed Fidel on Cuba's highest peak, Mt Turquino. The whole world could now see the rebels at work.

Fidel, though, was almost left behind by events in Havana. His tiny band had actually accomplished very little compared with the Revolutionary Directorate whose bombings and sabotage were gradually weakening Batista's control. On 13 March they attempted their boldest strike: a heavily armed group attacked the presidential palace, killed the guards and penetrated to Batista's office. The president barely escaped to the third floor by a concealed lift. Meanwhile, Echeverría had burst into the radio station and broadcast a manifesto. The army moved in instantly, the students were captured or killed, and Echeverría himself was shot down on the street. This was the most drastic assault on the dictatorship so far. Had it succeeded, the urban rebels would have taken over and Fidel (who was not consulted in the planning) left aside. Echeverría's death removed a radical hero whose popularity rivalled Fidel's.

The rebels were also active. In March, they were strengthened by fifty-eight recruits (including three Americans) brought in by Celia Sánchez and a sympathetic rice planter, Huber Matos. On 28 May the enlarged force successfully stormed the base at El Uvero west of Santiago, capturing a truck and badly needed supplies. With this victory, Fidel showed that he could defeat the army. As a result, Batista withdrew the isolated garrisons, leaving the rebels free to move about the Sierra.

Fidel was as concerned with politics as with fighting. In July 1957 leaders of the Ortodoxos came to the mountains and joined in signing the Sierra Maestra Manifesto for free elections, constitutional government and agricultural reform. Although consistent with his announced policies, it may not have been what Fidel really had in mind, for Che (who regarded these sympathetic politicians as 'cavemen') wrote that this programme was simply a brief pause along the road to revolution, to be scrapped when necessary. Yet it established an equal alliance between Fidel and the party and sidelined the anti-communist Frank País, who wanted major changes in the rebel leadership. However, when the united opposition proposed that Fidel incorporate his forces into the army after the revolution, he responded with a blast. His typically uncompromising letter of 14 December rejected any form of coalition, demanded civil government after the revolution, and named judge Manuel Urrutia as provisional president. Urrutia had endeared himself to Fidel by acquitting the captured survivors of the *Granma* on the grounds that revolt against a dictatorship was not a crime. The parties, except the Revolutionary Directorate, accepted the terms that made Fidel the undisputed leader of the revolution.

Meanwhile, other potential rivals had also fallen. The fourth anniversary of Moncada, on 26 July, passed in strange silence in Havana where the regime failed to prevent rebel flags from flying over some of the tallest buildings. In Santiago the police were carrying out a house-to-house search for Frank País. They finally caught and killed him on the 30th. His funeral the next day was the scene of demonstrations embarrassingly witnessed by the new US ambassador, and followed by a general strike especially effective in Oriente. Once again, fate had removed a powerful and devoted organizer, competent to head a movement. In September when a bold attempt by naval rebels to take over the city of Cienfuegos failed, Fidel was saved from a more serious kind of competition, for a successful military coup would have left him on the sidelines.

The unvanquished revolutionary, Fidel, started to get unexpected support. Beginning in September the American CIA channelled $50,000 to the 26 July Movement. As American public opinion swerved to the hero, the government was starting to hedge its bets. So were the communists, who at first had ignored or opposed Fidel since they followed the Soviet line of only supporting revolution based on the urban proletariat. In October a member of the Central Committee made the pilgrimage to the Sierra, and communists were authorized to join the movement, which they had already been supporting through their rural networks since the spring.

By the end of his first year in the Sierra Fidel controlled an organized territory. The rebels had a mountain base with a hospital, leather workshop, butcher and cigar factory, and issued a mimeographed newspaper. They slept in wooden shacks or hammocks and rarely bathed. They could be recognized by their inevitable beards and scruffy olive drab uniforms. At first they lived on vegetables, chicken soup and the occasional pig, but eventually came to terms with the peasants who would grow what they needed and with merchants in the towns at the base of the mountains. Supplies entered the roadless mountains by mule train through villages that served as bases for observers who could quickly spot a stranger or suspicious activity. All goods were paid for. Weapons, though, were a serious problem, for the army blockaded the mountains. Nevertheless, some got through, the greatest quantity left over from the attack on the presidential palace. Che Guevara described the daily life of the rebels in his detailed and often moving diary. He recounts with some feeling how his band was forced to kill their mascot, a puppy that wouldn't stop barking; yet he showed no such remorse for the execution of human beings.

Fidel's greatest helper was Celia Sánchez who moved to the Sierra and shared his bed in the tiny mountain headquarters. Practical, efficient, very popular and a devoted guerrilla, she took over business matters, bills and correspondence, with careful attention to the details that bored Fidel. She remained his soulmate and companion for many years. Otherwise, Fidel was closest to Raúl, Che and Camilo Cienfuegos, a worker from Havana who had joined the urban struggle before coming to Mexico and sailing on the *Granma*.

Isolated in the remote mountains, Fidel could make his voice heard after the rebels acquired a short-wave transmitter in February 1958. Soon everyone in Cuba could hear the sonorous announcement: 'This is Rebel Radio broadcasting from the Sierra Maestra in the Free Territory of Cuba.' The radio became a major and popular means of spreading publicity and demoralizing the government. So did interviews with the foreign press. Articles in the American popular magazines *Coronet* and *Look* portrayed Fidel as devoted to democracy and free enterprise, opposed to nationalizing land or industry. The American public never questioned these statements, nor his false claims that he had 1,000 men and controlled a population of 50,000.

Batista, meanwhile, had real problems. Although his overwhelming military strength allowed him to reject compromise or negotiation, he knew that force would be necessary to repress the rebels and growing urban terrorism. He frequently suspended civil rights (as allowed by the constitution) but faced growing pressure from the Americans to restore democracy. Early in 1958 his support started to fall away. In February the Catholic bishops called for a national unity government, which would involve treating the rebels as equals and probably force Batista's resignation. This was a real shock, but nothing compared to President Eisenhower's suspension of military supplies in March. Although this made no practical difference, many saw it as the writing on the wall and started to temporize or drift away.

When the rebels and the civic resistance announced a general strike, Batista declared a national emergency and withdrew permanently to Camp Columbia. Fidel, who had about 200 men, responded by ordering all highway traffic stopped and sending parties out to round up cattle on the estates around the mountains. The 10,000 animals, distributed among the peasants, gave Castro an unexpected lesson: the undernourished peasants eventually ate them rather than concentrating on long-range production of meat and milk. His resultant distrust of their motives had important effects in the future.

When the general strike began on 9 April Fidel was at first elated, then horrified, as it became clear that poor organization and Batista's control over labour would make it collapse rapidly. He had counted on the strike as a certain route to power; instead, Batista gained the support of business and finance and believed that it was now his turn to win. In the aftermath, leaders of the Revolutionary Directorate went to the Sierra to face Fidel, who sacked most of them, and took personal control of all resistance. The Sierra was now unquestionably in charge of the war; the rebel army would lead the Revolution. Its commanders were still ruling Cuba thirty years later.

In May Batista launched 7,000 troops, most of them conscripts with no experience of fighting, against the Sierra. His aim was to push Fidel's forces back into an isolated corner were they could be smashed. The campaign began on 24 May and lasted seventy-six days. General Cantillo first advanced from the north, against the remote rebel head-quarters and the transmitter for Radio Rebelde. A month of skirmishing, however, got him nowhere, for the rebels commanded the heights, had infinitely superior intelligence (though only a fraction of the manpower) and knew every inch of the ground. Cantillo's troops operated at a tremendous disadvantage in unfamiliar steep and rough terrain. Even though they managed to occupy Santo Domingo just below the main rebel base, they could advance no further and withdrew with substantial losses in mid-June. Cantillo next tried attacking from the south, but was ambushed and forced to surrender in a campaign Fidel directed personally. Unlike the army, the rebels released all their captives unharmed, only keeping the weapons, a policy that enhanced their growing reputation. A final attack on Santo Domingo also failed. By August it was clear that the government had lost any hope of crushing the rebellion.

Batista still had no intention of giving up, but his support was collapsing. General Cantillo entered into negotiations with Fidel, who proposed he lead a coup, and the US State Department started making plans to replace Batista, believing that a rebel victory would be a worse alternative. Castro, though, had no more use for the Americans than for compromise. After a rocket attack by US-built planes, he wrote, 'The Americans are going to pay dearly for what they are doing. When this war is over, a much wider war will begin for me, the war I will wage against them.'[4]

Meanwhile, the war had spread beyond the Sierra. Since March 1958 Raúl's column had been operating in the mountains east of Biran. In June when he controlled most of the Oriente countryside, he suddenly kidnapped fifty Americans to force the government to call off its air attacks. The US sent consular officials to negotiate directly with Raúl, bypassing and further humiliating Batista. Having made his point, he released them unharmed. Raúl, far more than Fidel, waged an ideological war: he carried out land reform and indoctrinated his officers and troops in Marxism. They later formed the core of a new national army. Ever since the general strike, the communists had been gaining influence, for their organized network could support the rebels in the cities; they now maintained a permanent representative in the Sierra.

In August, fresh from victory and in conscious imitation of the heroes of 1895, Fidel despatched two columns. Camilo's was to reach the far west, and Che's the centre, where he was to cut the island in half, securing control of Oriente. After six weeks of painful marching, Che reached the Escambray mountains where he found other resistance groups active. With much effort and persuasion, he took over from them and started blockading the cities.

The widely boycotted elections that Batista held in November were meaningless as his regime started to disintegrate. Fidel moved out of the Sierra for the first time and captured the major town of Palma Soriano. United Fruit, worried about a rebel threat to burn the cane fields, appealed to Eisenhower, who sent a special emissary to persuade Batista to resign. This was one of several last-ditch efforts to set up a regime that would not include Fidel. On Christmas Eve, Fidel returned to Birán for a feast, then met General Cantillo who agreed to revolt and turn the government over to him. By now, Castro's nominee Urrutia had arrived from Venezuela with a shipment of arms. They were hardly needed. On New Year's Day 1959 Santa Clara fell to Che's blockade and Santiago surrendered to Fidel. But the night before, after a sombre party, Batista had flown away. Cantillo informed the American ambassador the next day, and the news spread rapidly. The relieved population of Havana smashed parking meters, slot machines and the windows of American-owned hotels, but there was no bloodshed. The rebels had won.

TRANSFORMING CUBA, 1959–60

B atista had fled, but for the moment General
Cantillo held power. To stop him from setting
up a military junta, Fidel called a general strike,
which the people enthusiastically turned into a three-
day holiday. The army actually posed no problem;
Camilo and Che easily took over its bases in Havana.
The delirious population of Santiago received Fidel
on 2 January 1959. In the first of the mass assemblies
that became his hallmark, he told them that the
Revolution, now only beginning, would make Cuba
totally free – not like 1898 when the Americans took
control. The next day he began his slow triumphal
procession across the island.

Fidel and his warriors, with their beards, cigars and
army fatigues, rode jeeps and tanks for five days past
wildly adoring crowds. The liberator of Cuba stopped
to greet his admirers, address the people and make

sure his men were in control of local barracks and administrations. There was no resistance; in fact, people flocked to join the rebel army, and thousands appeared in an olive drab they had never worn.

On 8 January Fidel arrived in Havana. His first stop was at Echeverría's house, to show his appreciation for the urban rebels, and the first people he met were Naty and his son, Fidelito, who moved him to tears. The crowd magically opened for him as he entered the packed streets of the capital. That evening, at Camp Columbia, he addressed them. A flock of white doves was released to symbolize peace; when one of them miraculously perched on his shoulder, many believed that he was more than human. His extemporaneous speech (with his prodigious memory he often spoke for hours without notes) turned into a dialogue with the crowd, a technique he called 'direct democracy'. The subject was the Revolutionary Directorate, which had occupied the university. In a series of rhetorical questions, Fidel asked the crowds if the students needed weapons (No! No!) and whether he should agree to become commander-in-chief (Yes! Yes!). The Directorate surrendered its weapons that night; the last rival had succumbed.

President Urrutia put together a respectable cabinet, restored the constitution of 1940, and promised elections within eighteen months. The United States quickly recognized the new regime. Officially, Fidel was only commander of the army, which left him free to develop his own plans. In fact, he ran the whole show from his suite in the penthouse of the Hilton Hotel, renamed the Havana Libre, and in a beach house where the secret Office of Revolutionary Plans and Co-ordination met. Marxists were prominent among his advisers. With them, he worked out the agenda that he presented in mass meetings, on television and in interviews. The president and cabinet could only approve without discussion. On 13 February Fidel became prime minister and had the constitution (which had only been approved a week before) changed to allow him to direct policy. Urrutia, who was never consulted on anything important, became a mere figurehead.

Cuba was still full of Batista's henchmen, many of them real criminals. Fidel sent them before special revolutionary tribunals. Although this was never a bloodthirsty regime, the executions (which eventually reached 500) stirred denunciation in the American Senate. Fidel responded furiously that any

US intervention would cost the lives of 200,000 gringos. These remarks marked the beginning of the end for friendly relations with the American government. In February he consulted his massed supporters. When he asked the crowd what to do with war criminals, they enthusiastically answered 'To the wall!' The same month saw a vast public trial in Havana's main stadium of three especially brutal Batista commanders. Although they were plainly guilty, the atmosphere brought down an American jeer about a 'Roman circus' instead of justice. In fact, justice soon took a real beating. In March a tribunal in Santiago acquitted forty-four of Batista's aviators. A disgusted Fidel demanded a new trial on the grounds that 'revolutionary justice is based not on legal principles but on moral conviction'.[1] When the aviators were sentenced, the rule of law came to an end.

The American public, still wild for the revolutionary hero, did not share its government's suspicions. On 15 April Fidel left for Washington at the invitation of the Society of Newspaper Reporters. The students at Princeton and Harvard loved him, and he made a great hit in New York where he announced new slogans of 'bread without terror' and 'revolutionary humanism'. Only Vice-President Nixon, who met him in place of a conveniently absent Eisenhower, was not impressed. By this time the National Security Council was already talking about replacing Fidel, but few shared their fear that communism loomed in the Caribbean. They did not know that Raúl and his allies were firmly entrenched in the army and were taking over the vast popular militia, or that communist organizers were active in towns and villages.

Fidel had long demanded land reform. In power, he carried it out: 200,000 sharecroppers, squatters and tenants received deeds to the land they worked, confiscated from Cuban and American holdings. Fidel's passion for this reform made him choke with emotion at the mass rally on 8 May where he announced it, and Raúl had to continue. For a time, every phone operator in the country answered with 'agrarian reform works'. The peasants were overjoyed, even though they could not sell the land and had to grow the crops ordained by the National Institute for Agrarian Reform (INRA). This organization extended its control over the whole economy, financing construction, confiscating land

and building up its own army. Fidel used it as another means of bypassing the regular government.

On 16 July 1959 huge headlines, FIDEL RESIGNS! greeted the astonished public: Fidel was no longer prime minister (though he kept the army command). The next day he explained on TV that he could no longer work with Urrutia who was conspiring against the revolution. Vast crowds denounced the horrified president who resigned as he watched Fidel's speech. No evidence against him was ever produced. He fled to the Venezuelan embassy and on the 26th, the anniversary of Moncada, Fidel agreed to return to office, with the radical Osvaldo Dorticós as president. He had carried out a coup by television. His regime was taking firmer shape as revolutionaries replaced civil servants, and nationalizations and confiscations weakened the old power structure. Since the revolution was in charge and approved by constant mass meetings, there was no need for elections. They could be held, Fidel announced, only under suitable conditions, perhaps after four years. The crowds chanted 'Revolution First, Elections After!' The elections have never been held.

Urrutia was accused of participating in the 'conspiracy' of Cuba's first serious defector, Major

Díaz Lanz, commander of the air force. He had left in June, and denounced the growing communist influence before the US Senate. More seriously, in October, the devoted revolutionary Huber Matos resigned as governor of Camaguey province because of the communists in the army. Fidel flew into a rage and sent the reluctant Camilo to arrest him. In a passionate speech before a million spectators the Maximum Leader accused Matos of conspiring with Urrutia, Díaz Lanz and the United States to depose him. When he asked the crowd what he should do with Matos, they shouted back, 'To the wall!' Fidel restored the revolutionary courts and Raúl's men moved into the key ministries. At Matos' trial in December, Fidel was the chief accuser, speaking for seven hours. There was no need for evidence; Matos got twenty years.

Disloyalty was rare, though, for revolutionary enthusiasm still burned, guided by Fidel who rejected any public cult of personality (though he constantly appeared in the media). Raúl and Che were his closest collaborators. By now, Raúl commanded the armed forces where communists were gaining control, while Che was minister of industry and head of the national bank (he characteristically signed only

'Che' on the banknotes). Camilo, though, had disappeared: on 28 October, the plane bringing him back from Camaguey mysteriously crashed and was never recovered.

The traditionally turbulent university soon fell into line. Unsympathetic professors lost their jobs and the student elections in October took a new shape. Fidel appeared in person, demanding unanimity and ensuring that his man was elected head of the student union. Since then, for the first time in Cuba's history, there has been no opposition from the universities. Labour was next. When the unions held democratic elections in November, Fidel again demanded unity, with only one candidate for each office. Within a year most unions were run by communists or their allies. They, too, caused no further trouble. Nor did the youth, as the 26 July Movement absorbed their organizations.

So far, the revolution was not communist. The vast majority of the population had no desire for a communist society, and Castro knew that he had to tread carefully to avoid intervention from the United States. As late as July 1961 the credulous Herbert Matthews could write that Fidel was actually anti-communist. In fact, Cuba was drawing closer to the

Soviet Union. Camilo and Fidel had already received a high-ranking Soviet 'journalist' (KGB agent) in October 1959 and laid the groundwork for friendly relations. The following February Deputy Prime Minister Anastas Mikoyan arrived in Havana to open a trade fair. It was an enormous success, with a million Cuban visitors. Through Mikoyan, the Soviets agreed to buy a million tons of sugar and to establish diplomatic and cultural relations. Soon after, Cuba established the Juceplan (state planning) organization to co-ordinate all economic activity. Soviet-style central planning was beginning to take over. Not long after, the last moderate in the cabinet resigned, leaving the field free for the radicals.

The first two years were a time of tremendous military build-up as Fidel determined to protect himself from enemies at home and abroad. The army was doubled and augmented by a vast popular militia. Since Eisenhower's arms embargo was still in force, Fidel had to turn elsewhere. On 4 March 1960 a French freighter filled with Belgian ammunition exploded in Havana harbour, killing eighty-one people. Fidel rushed to the scene and accused the US of sabotage. In his speech honouring the dead, he created the revolution's most popular slogan: 'patria o muerte, venceremos!' 'Fatherland or death; we will win!' He may have been wrong about the ship, but by now the CIA was drawing up detailed plans to remove him.

Fidel had told the American newspapermen that 'the first thing dictators do is to finish the free press and establish censorship. There is no doubt that the free press is the first enemy of dictatorship'[2] Since Cuba still had a free press, the regime was subject to widespread criticism. The first step against it, in December 1959, involved inserting a postscript by pro-Castro journalists and printers at the end of each critical article. When the newspaper *Avance* refused to print them, it was closed, as were several other publications that could be linked with Batista. Havana's oldest and most respected paper, the conservative *Diario de la Marina*, succumbed in May 1960 when an armed mob invaded its premises. The police refused to act and 128 years of publication came to an abrupt end. The last independent paper closed two weeks later, and *Bohemia*, the immensely popular magazine that had given Fidel his best publicity, was taken over in July. The government also seized the radio and television stations. By the end of the year, when US papers were forbidden to circulate, the free press had come to a dead end, never to be restored. Dictatorship was looming in Cuba.

Dictators often slaughter their opponents. Fidel followed a much cleverer policy. After the first wave of executions, dissidents were free to leave. The first years of the revolution saw an unparalleled exodus of the upper and middle classes. Faced with nationalization, confiscation, ever more severe restrictions and growing economic problems, businessmen, doctors, lawyers and potential opponents poured out of the country. Most of them brought their bitter resentment to Miami. Eventually, over a million people – 10 per cent of the population – left. Fidel often used this safety valve to defuse discontent.

Revolutionary changes turned American suspicion into hostility, especially as Castro drew closer to the Soviets. Soviet interest in Cuba grew as their own relations with the US deteriorated. A shipload of Russian oil brought the first crisis in June 1960. Che ordered the American companies to refine it. When they refused, they were nationalized, and Cuba turned to the USSR for its fuel supplies. Soon after, Eisenhower cancelled the Cuban sugar quota. Khrushchev responded by increasing his purchases and rhetorically promised to stretch out a hand to the Cuban people and protect their revolution with rockets, if necessary. For the moment, nobody imagined that would ever happen.

Fidel returned to New York in September for one of his greatest theatrical triumphs. Before addressing the UN, he walked out of his hotel in a dispute about payment. His ostentatious move to the Theresa Hotel in Harlem, the famous black section of the city, gained phenomenal publicity. He took all his meals in his room, allowing the New York tabloids a field day reporting on the Cubans plucking chickens in the hotel, which also had other functions. The scantily clad ladies who worked there shocked the more puritanical of Fidel's entourage, but delighted others. They were no obstacle to a stream of radical world leaders who visited the hotel. Nasser and Tito, though, paled before Khrushchev himself who received a great bear hug. He told the massed reporters that he didn't know whether Fidel was a communist, but he was a *Fidelista*. The love feast with the Soviets had begun. The UN meeting, where Fidel gave the longest speech in its history, was almost an anticlimax, but it gave him the new role of international statesman.

On the day of his return Fidel announced the creation of his most potent organization, the Committees for the Defence of the Revolution (CDRs). These watchdog groups eventually embraced 80 per cent of the population, with headquarters on every street and in every settlement. Their job was ostensibly to maintain local security, but they reported all suspicious activities and people, as well as dissidence and complaints, to the growing secret police. It was soon impossible to advance in any way without attending meetings and getting a certificate from a committee; the CDRs became the regime's best means for controlling the population. Security, though, was necessary, for opposition was still active, especially in the Escambray mountains. Fidel personally led the first attack against the guerrillas after returning from New York. He sent in 100,000 of his new militia and followed Batista's detested policy of forcibly evacuating peasants, many of them to abandoned houses in Havana. The campaign gave the militia training that would soon be put to use.

Fidel naturally (and correctly) accused the United States of supporting the rebels, one more element in the increasing hostility. Since June the government had been nationalizing American properties at an alarming rate, beginning with the big hotels, with their Mafia-run casinos, then sugar mills, refineries and public utilities. The nationalizations were intended to benefit the population by eliminating profits and lowering the cost of living, while eliminating US control of the economy. Eisenhower, involved in a presidential campaign, had to act tough: on 13 October he banned all US exports to Cuba except medicine. The blockade had begun. Castro reacted immediately: on the 14th the INRA expropriated banks and 382 companies belonging to the Cuban bourgeoisie. The same day, the Urban Reform Law drastically reduced rents and allowed tenants to buy their apartments. American interests were badly hurt. Finally, on 29 October, the American ambassador was recalled, never to return. Cuba was free from US domination.

The Christmas of 1960 was like no other; public celebrations were banned and instead of the traditional nativity scenes there was a huge image of Fidel, Che and Juan Almeida (the highest-ranking black in the movement) as the Three Wise Men bearing gifts of Agrarian Reform, Urban Reform and Education. Camilo adorned the sky as an angel; the star was José Martí.

SIX

EXPERIMENTS IN REVOLUTION, 1961–70

The revolution named its years: 1961 was the Year of Education, as Fidel determined to eradicate illiteracy. Ten thousand classrooms sprouted while an enthusiastic army of students flocked to the country, to instruct the peasants. They used the manual *Venceremos* which taught people to spell words like Cuba, Fidel, Camilo and Raúl; the first phrase was 'La Reforma Agraria' and the first sentence 'the peasants work in the cooperative'. The campaign worked, but it had unexpected consequences. Many of the girl instructors, released from traditional restraints, came back pregnant. Breaking traditions included teaching children to obey the party more than their parents, and sending many of them to work in the fields.

The year began with a huge parade full of Soviet equipment and Fidel's speech denouncing 'worms' who had abandoned the revolution. He ordered the US to reduce its Havana staff drastically ('Throw them out!', clamoured the crowd). On 3 January Eisenhower broke diplomatic relations. That same month, the new president J.F. Kennedy inherited the plans to invade Cuba or, with the help of the Mafia, to assassinate Castro. As a preliminary, the CIA launched sabotage that consumed sugar fields, factories and stores, and attacked transport and military bases.

Preparations for the invasion were too poorly disguised to escape Fidel's efficient intelligence. He warned massed rallies of an impending attack and put the militia on alert. The original plan called for a force to be landed near Trinidad on the south coast, where they could make contact with the rebels in the Escambray. At the last minute, though, the landing was moved to the less populated Bay of Pigs, at the edge of a vast swamp which, as it happened, Fidel knew extremely well. At dawn on 15 April 1961, B26 bombers painted in Cuban colours attacked Cuba's airfields, but Fidel had hidden his best aircraft. The next day his funeral speech for those killed described a dying man who wrote 'Fidel' on the wall with his blood. Castro denounced cowardly and treacherous Americans and for the first time described the revolution as socialist, an announcement he had planned for May Day. Meanwhile, Kennedy fatally undermined the operation by refusing to provide air cover. Early on the 17th, boats borrowed from United Fruit deposited 1,500 Cuban exiles on the beaches, where they had to face an unexpected air attack. Fidel personally urged on the pilots, and rushed to the scene. With their supporting freighters sunk, the invaders were stranded, and surrendered after two days of hard fighting. Soviet weapons and tanks, the militia, and the loyalty of the population had won. The attackers were captured, brought to Havana and interrogated by Castro in the stadium. Few were executed; the rest were ransomed from imprisonment a year later. It was a tremendous humiliation for the United States, still commemorated in a billboard on the beach that reminds visitors of 'The First Defeat of Imperialism in America'.

The invasion had counted on popular support. On the day of the attack, however, security forces rounded up some 50,000 potential opponents.

Although most were released after the fighting, the sudden arrest of people from all parts of the society thoroughly cowed the population and broke the back of any future resistance. There was no uprising against Fidel; the revolution was still immensely popular, and Fidel's victory united the people behind him even more firmly.

The Bay of Pigs did not end the American threat. Kennedy was determined to destroy Castro, whose need for protection coincided with Khrushchev's fear of losing his new strategic ally. One possible solution was to station Soviet missiles in Cuba as a deterrent. In July 1962 Raúl and Khrushchev met in Moscow to discuss installing defensive weapons; plans for atomic missiles were probably also on the agenda. Later in the month, when Fidel was publicly predicting another American invasion, Soviet men and equipment started to arrive. US intelligence reported the activity, but the US government remained sceptical. In October, however, freighters unloaded atomic missiles and the greatest crisis of the Cold War began when US spy planes produced clear evidence that the missiles were being installed (they were manned by Russians, not Cubans). Kennedy, who could not look passive in the face of the forthcoming elections, announced to a tense public that he was sending the fleet to blockade Cuba. Many thought that nuclear war was at hand. Two days later, to the world's relief, Soviet ships heading for Cuba turned back. The immediate crisis was over, but the missiles remained. When Kennedy threatened to invade by the 30th, Khrushchev capitulated. In exchange for the withdrawal of American missiles from Turkey, he agreed to dismantle the Soviet missiles in Cuba. He also secured an informal promise that the Americans would not invade. In a sense, Khruschev's bluff succeeded, for he guaranteed security for the Cuban revolution at no cost to the Soviet Union.

Kennedy, however, had no intention of leaving Cuba alone. In 1963, the CIA continued to support sabotage and even open attacks. The popular *Life* magazine happily reported one of them in an adventure story entitled 'A Wild Fighting Ride on the Old Spanish Main'.[1] They coincided with advanced and sometimes fantastic plans against the Maximum Leader himself. Agents devised schemes to make Fidel's beard fall out, kill him with a poisoned cigar or diving suit, blow him up with an exploding seashell as he swam or, more practically, suborn a waiter to drop cyanide in his milkshake. In all this, the CIA had the co-operation of the Mafia, still smarting from the loss of their lucrative casinos. Castro, who knew exactly what was happening, issued a warning in September: 'US leaders should think that if they assist in terrorist plots to eliminate Cuban leaders, they themselves will not be safe.'[2] In November, Kennedy was assassinated. Among the innumerable explanations are those that name Cuba: that Castro turned a group sent to kill him against Kennedy, or that Lee Harvey Oswald, a great admirer of Cuba, acted in what he thought were Castro's interests. Nothing can ever be proved, but the suspicion lingers.

When Fidel learned that Khrushchev was withdrawing the missiles, he flew into a rage, kicking the walls and breaking a mirror. Relations with his Russian friends and the local communists remained difficult for a decade as he tried to bring the communists under his own control and to create an independent foreign policy. Ideology was not a problem: already on 1 December 1961 he announced: 'I am a Marxist-Leninist and shall remain so until the last days of my life,'[3] a statement that got him thrown out of the Organization of American

States. By then, he had created a monolithic party, the Integrated Revolutionary Organizations that the communists, with their superior organization, dominated. It became the Cuban Communist Party in October 1965, with Fidel as first secretary. By 1968, when he removed his last potential (and openly pro-Soviet) rivals, his personal dominance of State and Party was assured.

In the 1960s Fidel needed peace at home so he could deal with the Russians, whom he never forgave for their betrayal in the Missile Crisis. Relations took a turn for the better in April 1963 when he flew off for a grand tour of the Soviet Union. During his forty-day stay, he upset his hosts by insisting on walking unannounced through Red Square, but received a warmer reception than any foreigner since the Second World War. He reviewed the May Day parade at the Kremlin, toured the whole country and was lavishly entertained. He returned the following January for meetings where the Soviets guaranteed a high price for sugar and promised cheap oil in exchange. This helped Cuba's economy but increased dependence on Russia which expected a recalcitrant Castro to follow its policies. Despite an un-precedented visit by the new Russian leader Alexei

Kosygin in 1967, Fidel refused to attend the celebrations of the fiftieth anniversary of the Russian Revolution that November. Relations reached a new low.

Problems revolved around Fidel's determination to support revolutionary movements in Latin America and Africa, while the Russians insisted on working through local communist parties. Successful revolutions would give Fidel allies, weaken American global dominance, and allow him greater independence. His agent was Che Guevara, whose hopes of industrializing Cuba and replacing material with moral incentives were rapidly fading. Already in 1963 Che had been sent to Africa to establish guerrilla bases. But he became so disillusioned with tribal infighting that he gave up, and disappeared. After Fidel read Che's letter renouncing Cuban citizenship in October 1965, nothing was seen or heard of him. In fact, he had left secretly to stir revolution in Bolivia. His long campaign there, doomed by the opposition of Moscow and the local communists, and the lack of indigenous support, culminated in his death on 9 October 1967. The next week, Fidel mentioned him for the first time in two years. He instantly became a legend, the hero whose portraits soon decorated the rooms of radical western students and still adorn all Cuba. Che's death left Fidel as the only figure who commanded widespread affection.

When Fidel continued to preach revolution in Latin America, the Russians decided to teach him a lesson. Havana's traditional military parade of New Year 1968 had to be cancelled because of lack of fuel. The Russians were holding back deliveries at a time when Fidel had ambitious economic plans. With no alternative source of aid, he could not resist for long. Consequently, when the Russians invaded Czechoslovakia in August 1968, Castro was one of the few world leaders to support them. At the end of the year, he agreed to abandon revolution in Latin America. Oil deliveries increased and Cuba returned to the Soviet embrace.

Castro showed in 1968 that he was not about to allow a 'Prague Spring' in Cuba. In fact, he had been bringing his own people under ever tighter control for years. Repression began with the mass arrests during the Bay of Pigs, soon followed by 'Operation P' against pimps, prostitutes and pederasts. In both cases, information from the CDRs led the security forces into private homes. Intimidation grew as the economic situation declined. The US blockade, incompetent central planning, huge military expenses and the exodus of the professionals produced constant shortages and deteriorating conditions, especially in Havana. Fidel had no love for the bourgeois capital but directed resources to the countryside, where roads, water supply and housing brought real improvements. Nevertheless, in April 1962, a huge crowd of housewives in the town of Cardenas, most of them poor and black, marched for food and against communism. Fidel sent in the tanks, crushing the last public demonstration against the revolution. He had also attacked the church after the US invasion, closing religious schools and expelling dozens of priests. Catholics were forbidden to join the Party. Jehovah's Witnesses and other sects followed. In 1965 came the turn of rebellious teenagers and homosexuals, who were sent off to re-education camps where they received extremely rough treatment.

Cultural dissent also suffered. In 1961 the most popular literary review in Latin America, *Lunes de Revolución*, was closed. Fidel, his pistol on the table, presided over the trial of the editors and writers accused of being counter-revolutionary. From now on, his principle of 'within the revolution everything, against the revolution nothing' prevailed. Yet at the same time, the government produced huge quantities of books: people could read all the approved literature they wanted. Cuba was still remarkable in the Soviet bloc for the freedom of expression its experimental artists and poets enjoyed, a feature that attracted sympathetic European intellectuals. That, too, ended in 1968 when the internationally famed poet Heberto Padilla, whose poems of disillusion had won a major Cuban prize, was denounced and forbidden to publish. By then, though, Fidel had opened the safety valve again. In September 1965 he told the CDRs that anyone who wanted to leave was free to go. Thousands suddenly appeared at the small port of Camarioca; President Johnson promised to receive them. Although they had surrendered all valuables and lost their jobs and ration cards while waiting for transport, they left. Two of Fidel's sisters went with them.

Fidel kept his personal life strictly private, even maintaining, as he wrote to Naty in 1954, 'you know that personal matters are the least important to me'.[4] His family was last publicly mentioned when his mother died in August 1963. Although Raúl wept,

Fidel showed no outward emotion; the old lady had never forgiven him for burning her cane fields during the revolution. Other ties were also broken. Soon after the revolution, Mirta emigrated to Spain, reluctantly leaving Fidelito in his father's charge. Naty was doomed to disappointment. For a couple of years, Fidel continued to see her, but soon ended the relationship, though he did occasionally visit their daughter Alina. Like Teresa Casuso, Naty ran up against the wall that Celia built around Fidel. Celia no longer had a romantic relation with Fidel, but she kept out other women who might have a claim, while admitting casual one-night stands. There were plenty of them. Although flattered by the leader's attentions, some complained that he didn't remove his cigar or boots during their encounters, or even worse, wanted only to talk politics. Celia saw to it that they received presents on their birthdays. By 1962 or '63, Fidel had started another family, with a dark-eyed beauty, Delia Soto, by whom he eventually had five sons. But the public knew nothing of that.

Nor did they know where he lived. During the early years of the revolution, he moved between the Havana Libre, Celia's and other apartments in Havana and his beach house. Later, he was reputed to have a couple of mansions, a hunting estate and an entire luxurious island where he received foreign visitors and conducted financial affairs. In all this, he maintained the restless habits of the guerrilla, while protecting himself from the very real threat of assassination.

Fidel wanted to diversify the economy by ending Cuba's dependence on sugar, but attempts to substitute industry failed from lack of funds and the need to produce sugar to pay for Russian oil. In his effort to gain economic independence, he launched the country on a series of wild experiments, often the result of reading that made him believe he had discovered novel solutions. His ideal was a rural society with organized communes where the state, rather than the family, would raise the children. The family, like private property, would become superfluous. Private enterprise, in any case, was doomed. In March 1968 Fidel launched an offensive against the last vestiges of capitalism. After denouncing people who hung around bars and fried food stalls, he shut down private shops, bars, garages and every other place where people gathered. This supposedly freed workers for agriculture and industry, but actually caused massive disruption and high prices. Sullen resignation set in as the vibrant street life of Havana and other cities came to an end.

Raising agricultural production was Fidel's special dream. Reforms in 1963 restricted private farms to 67 acres; their owners were tightly controlled. The rest were organized into huge state farms on the Soviet model. They became the subject of Fidel's enthusiasm, which began with the cows. Fidel decided that imported Holstein cattle could be crossbred with the local beasts to produce the new F1 ('F' for 'Fidel') breed ideally suited to local conditions and capable of producing great quantities of milk. The whole country was awash with propaganda; prize bulls got air-conditioned stalls and every cow that died had to be reported to the police. By the end of the decade, though, the project had flopped, along with an attempt to grow a new feed that the cattle refused to eat. So did the massive effort to plant a green belt of coffee and fruit trees around Havana. In 1968 thousands of conscripts and volunteers joined the effort whose failure the farmers, quite rightly, had foretold.

Fidel's most grandiose campaign involved sugar, where he wanted to increase production from 1963's feeble 3.5 million tons. He decided that Cuba could produce 10 million tons in 1970 by mobilizing the population. The million faithful who flocked to Revolution Plaza on 2 January 1969 learned that the next harvest would extend for twelve months instead of the usual three, and that they would have no holidays until it was over. Even Christmas was postponed, not to be celebrated again for thirty years. Workers, students, the young and the old, and foreign volunteers went off to cut cane amid tremendous enthusiasm. Here was the answer to Cuba's problem. Fidel himself took up the machete; so did 700 Russian sailors and the whole staff of the Soviet embassy. Virtually all other activities stopped; the population worked under military discipline while Fidel pored over maps and reports. By January 1970 500,000 volunteers had brought in the first million tons; the government announced that saboteurs would be shot. The traditional January celebrations were cancelled, and the working day extended to ten hours, but the harvest fell inexorably behind. Bad weather, faulty equipment, fire and blight conspired to keep the yield to a rational 8.5 million tons. There were no celebrations. Instead, Fidel denounced lazy workers and announced new rationing, but when he offered to resign, the crowd shouted 'No! No!'

A decade of revolution had produced a new Cuba. Private enterprise was gone, public services and transport were erratic if they existed at all, Havana and other cities were increasingly dirty and shabby. Consumer goods and even many basic foods were impossible to find. Yet the country was dotted with new hospitals, schools and roads. Slums disappeared as functional new housing sprouted around towns and villages. People might not be able to express themselves freely, but they had access to free education and medical care. Unemployment had virtually disappeared. For every malcontent, there were hundreds still enthusiastic for the revolution, despite the disappointments of the age of experiment.

SEVEN

MOSCOW'S MAN IN HAVANA, 1970–89

A Cuban joke of the 1980s explained that Cuba was the biggest country in the world: it had its president in Havana, its army in Angola and its capital in Moscow. In fact, during these decades Fidel gained renown as champion of the Third World while his country rested in the Soviet embrace.

The failure of the ten-million-ton harvest forced Cuba closer to Russia. Disruption of the economy meant greater dependence on foreign aid, which had only one source. Soviet influence came to dominate every aspect of society and government. Heads rolled after the disaster: ministers were sacked and government personnel replaced. By the end of 1970 more than half the cabinet were army officers and a special Soviet-Cuban Commission effectively took control of the economy. In 1972, Cuba officially joined the Moscow's eastern bloc trade organization, Comecon. Fidel denounced loafers and absentees as the Russian presence became ever stronger. Soviet technicians advised on agriculture and industry and managed to introduce more order, but they had little contact with the Cuban public. Although Russian replaced English in the schools, Cubans met their Soviet allies only on formal occasions or through the black market where the Russians seemed willing to trade anything for alcohol.

The arrest of the poet Padilla in 1971 signalled a new wave of repression of intellectuals. Fidel condemned all expressions of bourgeois ideology, demanding that art must serve the revolution and Marxism. A new National Cultural Council under a former army officer made sure that it did. Meanwhile, the Interior Ministry organized a central population registry that gave the government full information on every citizen. The CDRs did the rest. Primary schoolchildren in uniforms studied their Soviet textbooks and marched under the slogan Study, Work, Rifle; all those over the age of six were supposedly engaged in some form of productive labour. At the same time, there was no unemployment and the people were healthier and better educated than ever before.

Fidel's experiments continued, though on a reduced scale. He always hoped to improve the economy which suffered from wild swings in the price of sugar (85 cents per pound in 1974, 8 in 1976). Tourism was one possibility; new hotels accommodated increasing numbers of foreigners who were kept rigidly segregated from the population. Under the liberal Carter regime, tourism from the US also seemed a possibility. In 1979 Fidel welcomed 100,000 Miami Cubans (the 'worms' he had long denounced). Unfortunately, the plan backfired when the population learned that their cousins in Florida, far from being desperate refugees who sent their daughters out to prostitution, were rich, well-dressed and condescending. He opened the doors under different circumstances in 1980. On 1 April a truckload of dissidents crashed through the gates of the Peruvian embassy. Suddenly, 10,000 Cubans filled the grounds, demanding to leave. On May Day Fidel denounced them as 'scum' and encouraged the CDRs to attack. The following weeks were marked by violent clashes between loyalists and the people Castro was allowing to leave. Since the US agreed to take all of them, he emptied his jails of criminals, lunatics and homosexuals, who joined the flotilla that eventually transported 120,000 from the port of Mariel. Most of them, though, represented a cross-section of Cuban society. Once again, the safety valve worked, defusing discontent and ironically causing a major crime wave in Miami.

Generally, this was a notable period under an increasingly Soviet-style government. Although Fidel and the veterans of the Sierra still held the highest offices, the regime took on a new shape. The presidency was abolished in 1972 (Dorticós became head of the national bank) and military men dominated the Council of Ministers. They controlled the judicial system and the army, now reorganized to conform with socialist countries. The old revolutionaries gave up their rank of *comandante* (major) to become generals. The new constitution, approved by the Party's First Congress in 1975, followed the Soviet model. It provided for a Council of Ministers and Politburo, but with a Cuban innovation: the local organizations of popular power that were, at least in theory, freely elected (the party chose the candidates). Fidel was Head of State, First Secretary of the Communist Party, President of the

Council of State and of the Council of Ministers and Commander-in-Chief of the army. The constitution granted rights to education, health and employment and guaranteed equality between husbands and wives. At every level, the party, with its inflexible discipline, was supreme.

Secure at home, Fidel could embark on the most brilliant epoch of his foreign ventures. Friendship with the USSR and diminished hostility from the USA allowed him to profit from opportunities and to extend his influence from Central America to Africa. The decade began and ended well: Fidel's ally Salvador Allende took power in Chile in 1970 and his protégé Daniel Ortega gained control of Nicaragua in 1979, but the election of Ronald Reagan in 1980 soon left Fidel's foreign ambitions in tatters.

Salvador Allende, a good friend of Cuba, promised to be a valuable ally. He gave Fidel an enthusiastic welcome when he arrived in November 1971 for a visit that lasted twenty-five days. Travelling throughout the country, he preached the virtues of socialism and the Soviet alliance to large crowds. The only problems came when Fidel realized he could not talk as long as he liked and actually had to face heckling and hostile comments in the press; that never happened in Cuba. Although he was the revolutionary and Allende the parliamentarian, Fidel sensibly cautioned his friend not to antagonize the army or the United States and not to abolish private enterprise. Towards the end of his stay, he encountered a massive demonstration of women banging pots and pans, demanding better living conditions and telling him to go home. He went away more convinced than ever that an opposition was highly undesirable. Allende returned the visit a year later, but succumbed to a coup (he supposedly shot himself with the machine gun Fidel had given him) in September 1973. Allende joined the pantheon of Cuba's heroes, but his fall, reputedly provoked by the United States, was a tremendous blow.

Fidel's next long trip, in May and June 1972, took him to ten countries. The first stop was Africa, which he perceived as ripe for a revolution guided by Cuba. Eastern Europe meant cheers and receptions, though the Poles, who preferred being friends with the west, were notably cool. In Moscow, Premier Kosygin awarded him the Order of Lenin. When he returned to Moscow in December, he met the other communist rulers, who treated him as an equal. Fidel addressed the Supreme Soviet, and received great concessions: the Soviets agreed to double the price of sugar, and postponed payment of Cuba's debt till 1986. By now, Cuba was receiving one-third of the aid Russia gave to the entire Third World, as well as half the military aid.

The Russians had reason to be happy. When Fidel attended the conference of Non-Aligned Nations in 1973, he attacked the US and praised the Soviets. Libya's Qaddafi was one of many who questioned this kind of 'non-alignment', but an embrace replaced suspicion when Fidel suddenly broke relations with Israel and became a prime backer of the PLO. Later in the year, he sent Cuban troops to help Syria fight Israel. The next January Premier Brezhnev himself came to Cuba. During his week's stay, he visited the Moncada barracks and joined Fidel in addressing the masses in Revolution Plaza. The president of Mexico and the prime minister of Canada soon followed. Even the United States was starting to sound friendly. After the fall of Castro's enemy Nixon, American senators visited Cuba to explore possibilities and President Ford considered relaxing policy. His successor Jimmy Carter allowed more opening. Journalists flocked to Havana, where Fidel charmed and impressed them with his knowledge of American politics. Events in Africa and Latin America, though, prevented any real détente.

In April 1974 leftist revolutionaries who seized power in Portugal announced that its African colonies would be freed the next year. The three factions in Angola immediately began jockeying for supremacy. One had US backing, another turned to South Africa, but the Marxist MPLA occupied the capital, Luanda. The MPLA knew Cuba through Che's patronage of African liberation ten years before. They were also friendly with the Soviet Union which had shipped weapons but now refused the necessary manpower to avoid conflict with the US. Instead, Fidel stepped in. His natural sympathy with Africa combined with a good opportunity to give his army training in real combat. Since he was also from the Third World and could send an army that was largely black, his help was especially welcome. By November 1975, Cubans were pouring in, thanks to close co-ordination with the Soviets who supplied planes, ships and heavy weapons. Fidel personally supervised every stage of the operation, following the fighting on huge maps in his office and telephoning orders. Luanda and the MPLA were saved, but opposition remained strong in the countryside. Cuban forces remained in Angola; of the 300,000 who eventually served there, 20,000 never returned. In addition, Fidel sent many doctors, teachers and technicians. Since Angola paid for this assistance (ironically with revenues from Gulf oil), Castro's enemies labelled the Cubans 'mercenaries'.

Fidel embarked for Africa again in February 1977. After reviewing the troops in Angola, he flew to Somalia, where Cubans had long been training guerrillas and to Ethiopia which had just established a Marxist government. The two were in a bitter fight over contested territory. They were also part of the Cold War, for the Soviets, who originally supported Somalia, switched to Ethiopia. So did Fidel, who became friends with the Ethiopian leader Mengistu. In March 1978, the Cuban population learned that its army had been fighting in East Africa since January. An operation closely co-ordinated with Russia pushed the Somalis out of Ethiopia but earned Fidel widespread disdain since he was so obviously helping the Soviets and violating his principle of self-determination, for the contested area was inhabited by Somalis. His budding relationship with the United States was severely damaged, as was his friendship with Muslim nations when he obediently endorsed the Soviet invasion of Afghanistan in December 1979.

Fidel's sons participated in his romance with the Soviets. Fidelito and Jorge Angel were sent to study nuclear physics in Russia, soon followed by the five sons of Delia Soto. Fidelito acquired a Russian wife and eventually returned to head Cuba's nuclear commission. For a time, it appeared that he was being groomed to succeed his father, but he lost the job after the fall of the Soviet Union. Fidel, in fact, avoided nepotism; except for Raúl, none of his brothers or sisters ever gained high positions, nor did the rest of his children.

Fidel's activities gained international recognition. He was elected chairman of the non-aligned movement, effectively becoming chief spokesman for the Third World, and proudly presided over its 1979 conference in Havana. Many, of course, wondered how non-alignment could be so openly pro-Soviet. In March, Fidel's disciple Maurice Bishop seized power in Grenada. Cuban workers soon arrived to build an airport conveniently located on the route to Africa. Central America offered the next and best hope. For some time, Fidel had been encouraging the Sandinista rebels in Nicaragua. Since openly sending troops could lead to conflict with the United States, he confined himself to advising and co-ordinating. His efforts paid off when his protégés took over in July 1979. A month later, the Nicaraguan leader Daniel Ortega sat with Fidel on the reviewing stand for the Moncada anniversary. During the first year of its Marxist regime, Managua welcomed Fidel several times. The Sandinistas imitated Cuban uniforms, slogans and policies. Fidel hoped to make Nicaragua a base for undermining US influence in the region.

For Fidel, the election of Ronald Reagan in 1980 marked the beginning of a decade that culminated in disaster. Reagan had no use for communism; he agreed with his UN representative who called Fidel a 'Piltdown Man' (i.e. both antiquated and phoney). Reagan's Radio Martí beamed infuriating propaganda, while his government attacked leftist movements in the Americas and Soviet power everywhere. To make matters worse, the Cuban economy stubbornly refused to perform. Ambitious targets for sugar production were never met, and prices continued to fluctuate wildly while expenses mounted: huge amounts of aid flowed to Nicaragua and the debt to the Soviet Union inexorably increased. Faced with a growing American threat, Fidel increased his army and militia to a million men, the largest, best-equipped (and most expensive) in Latin America.

Fidel's personal life suffered a real blow in January 1980 when Celia Sánchez died. Well-organized and stable, she had been by his side since the Sierra days, and her apartment had been a valued refuge. Now he was on his own, though Raúl's wife Vilma Espín functioned as a kind of first lady. His own companion and mother of his sons, Delia, always stayed in the background.

In 1980 Fidel allowed farmers to sell their products on the free market. When that worked all too well, he cracked down on profiteers and pushed the farmers into co-operatives. His constant denunciations of inefficiency and incompetent bureaucrats culminated in the Rectification Campaign announced at the Party Congress in 1986. He attacked corruption and materialism, demanding a return to the egalitarian and moral values of the revolution. He called for sacrifice, more production and less consumption. With a core of advisers, he constantly travelled to investigate and intervene in every aspect of the economy, but without fundamental change, little improvement was possible.

Meanwhile, Reagan meant business. In 1983 he invaded Grenada, ending its Marxist experiment, and sending Fidel's workers packing. By open and covert means, he supported the anti-Sandinista forces in Nicaragua. Their success in elections that the overconfident Ortega allowed in 1990 finished off another Cuban ally. This was a real blow to Fidel, and confirmed his dislike of free elections. But these setbacks were as nothing compared with the news from the east.

As late as 1984 Fidel could boast that the Soviet Union was 'the fundamental pillar of our present and future'.[1] Not for long. In March 1985 Mikhail Gorbachev came to power, faced with the urgent need for fundamental reforms. *Glasnost* and *perestroika*, the watchwords of the day, were inimical to Fidel, but in 1986 he faithfully visited Moscow, where the speeches were routine. On his return, he tried some limited *glasnost* of his own, encouraging citizens to criticize ministers, but there was no question of changing the system. By 1988 he was openly criticizing Gorbachev, foreseeing quite correctly that too much reform would destroy socialism altogether. His new slogan for the thirtieth anniversary of the revolution, 'Socialism or death', showed where he stood. Nevertheless, smiles and huge crowds greeted Gorbachev when he arrived in

Havana in April 1989. Although he and Fidel signed a 25-year friendship treaty, the reality was harsh. The Russian announced that Cuba would have to start negotiating directly with its Soviet suppliers and that subsidies would be reduced. Worse was to come.

The changing dynamics of great power relations effectively removed Fidel from the international stage. After Cubans defeated the South Africans in Angola in April 1988, the USA and USSR co-operated in a treaty that officially brought Cuban troops home after thirteen years. The next year, President Bush invaded Panama, eliminating one of Fidel's most unsavoury allies. Both Angola and Panama were the background of a scandal that made the decade end on a sour note.

In June 1989 Cubans were horrified by headlines about Judicial Case no. 1. Cuba's greatest hero, General Arnaldo Ochoa, was on trial for treason together with some of Fidel's closest associates. Ochoa, who had fought at the Bay of Pigs, commanded the Cubans in Ethiopia and Angola. One of the few generals who was widely known and liked, he was on familiar terms with Fidel. In Angola, though, he had openly criticized Fidel's military strategy. After he returned to Cuba in January 1989, his disparaging remarks about Fidel's abilities as a commander and the regime's neglect of returning veterans reached Raúl who immediately suspected a conspiracy and had him arrested. There was a problem, though: Ochoa was not guilty of anything.

Fidel found the solution as the investigation reached his friends, the de la Guardia twins. One of them had been smuggling ivory and diamonds in Angola. More seriously, the other, Tony, was involved in the drug trade, using his position as head of the secret office Cuba maintained in Panama for selling visas, laundering money and smuggling US goods to Cuba. His close contacts with the Colombian drug cartels, who channelled money to South American guerrilla movements in exchange for permission to fly over Cuba, gave Tony de la Guardia the lucrative idea of allowing drugs to be flown into Cuba for transshipment to Florida. Raúl's agents soon discovered the plot; Fidel put the evidence to good use. He had Ochoa accused of involvement with the de la Guardias in the drug trade, and used it as an excuse to purge the whole Interior Ministry. Their chiefs, who lived in far greater luxury than Raúl's army commanders, were privy to too many secrets and could be a real danger if there ever were a conspiracy. The result was a televised court-martial; Fidel brought the charges; Ochoa, Tony de la Guardia, and several others confessed and were shot; the Interior Ministry was taken over by Raúl's men. All Cuba learned that no one, not even the highest, was safe: there could be no deviation or opposition while Cuba's allies were collapsing.

EIGHT

STAYING AFLOAT, 1990–9

The 1990s were the second heroic period of Fidel's career. He kept Cuba afloat despite economic collapse and against the eager anticipations of his enemies. Articles, books and seminars with titles like *Castro's Final Hour* or 'Is 1995 the Last Dance for Castro?' totally underestimated a leader who was capable of striking innovation and adaptation to unpredictable disaster.

The collapse of the Soviet Union and the ever-tightening American blockade threatened the end of communist Cuba. In 1991, Moscow, faced with a desperate need to retrench, concluded a trade agreement that offered a year's transition before cash replaced subsidy in its dealings with Cuba. Then there was a moment of hope: the coup of August 1991 that ousted Gorbachev reportedly delighted Castro's staff. But gloom soon followed as Yeltsin, who had no use for Cuba, triumphed. A month later, Gorbachev announced the withdrawal of Soviet troops from Cuba without consulting Fidel. They left in 1993, but by then the Soviet Union was no more.

Fidel tried, with increasing success through the decade, to establish friendly relations with Latin America and Europe. He travelled frequently near and far, getting moral and sometimes economic support. But few were willing to follow Canada, France and Spain in defying the United States. He even returned to New York in 1995, addressing the UN for a record six minutes (instead of hours) and sentimentally revisiting Harlem where he still had friends. Ever since the Revolution, and through all these years, he championed the poor countries of the Third World against the rich West, a position he has never abandoned.

Fidel also started to court the Church: in 1991 Catholics were allowed to join the Party and security agents disappeared from churches. Reconciliation moved through slow stages which included public outdoor masses, restoration of church buildings and quiet negotiations. In 1997 Christmas was openly celebrated for the first time in thirty years. Finally, in January 1998, the Pope arrived. His mass in

Revolution Square attracted huge crowds of the faithful, curious and dissident (wearing crosses had become a subtle sign of discontent among youth who had no knowledge of Christianity). Although the Pope urged greater freedom for Cubans, his denunciation of the US embargo pleased Fidel.

None of this, though, could compensate for the end of Soviet subsidies. For decades, the USSR had been pouring in money, paying high prices for sugar and shipping cheap fuel. Cuba had been costing the Russians $12 million a day; Cuba eventually owed them $18.3 billion. Even after 1993, there were residual agreements to exchange sugar for oil (the Russians were still willing to pay for electronic spy facilities in Cuba), but these failed to flourish as bad weather and poor organization reduced the harvest. In 1994, it produced only 3.3 million tons, the lowest in fifty years. As a result, anything that could generate cash was exported. Goods disappeared from the state shops where Cubans got their meagre rations, and the population sank into poverty.

Castro responded with the Special Period in Time of Peace, a series of emergency measures that drastically cut subsidies and production. If necessary, Cuba would revert to the Zero Option, where people would go back to the country and oxen and windmills would provide energy. In fact, oxen were soon pulling ploughs, while horsecarts and bicycles became major forms of transport as buses disappeared for lack of fuel and spare parts. Consumer goods were non-existent and even food drastically scarce. By 1992, the average calorie intake of Cubans had dropped to 900, far below any recognized standard. By then, exports had fallen by 60 per cent and imports by 70 per cent; economic activity was a shadow of what it had been three years before.

Castro's enemies gloated as the Americans moved to finish him off. In 1992, the so-called Cuban Democracy Act tightened the economic blockade, though it did allow more cultural exchange. Two years later, the US government severely restricted travel, forbade families from sending money to Cuba and ended the automatic right of asylum. This was in response to a new wave of refugees. On 5 August the first riots in thirty-six years had struck Havana: protesting mobs threw stones at the police and broke windows. People could no longer tolerate the shortages. Castro responded by opening the safety valve. His police looked the other way while 32,000 people sailed off on makeshift rafts. About 1,000 of them drowned.

The US Congress wanted to isolate and destroy Castro, but President Clinton was less motivated. In 1995, he eased many restrictions, but the following February brought another crisis: on Castro's personal orders, the Cuban air force shot down two small American planes. They belonged to the anti-Castro Brothers to the Rescue group that had already dropped leaflets over Havana. As a result, Congress passed the Helms-Burton Act which made the embargo permanent and provocatively allowed US citizens to sue foreign businesses that profited from property confiscated from Americans. It was to remain in effect until Cuba was a democracy, without Fidel or Raúl. As Senator Helms announced, he didn't care whether Fidel left Cuba in a horizontal or vertical position. The Americans remained on the warpath, accusing Cuba of involvement in the drug trade. After the Pope's visit, the situation eased, but by then Fidel had put the country back on the road to recovery.

In fact, Cuba was no threat to the United States or anyone else. Soviet troops and weapons were gone and the local military was in very poor shape. By 1995, the army was only at half strength. Shortages of fuel and ammunition meant inadequate training and low morale. Fully 75 per cent of the air force was out of commission, and the navy was being dismantled. Cuba no longer had access to foreign intelligence. Even the network of defensive tunnels Fidel had ordered dug when the Soviets pulled out were used for storing weapons and growing mushrooms. The only danger from Cuba might be another flood of refugees.

Fidel had no intention of letting his people starve. The Special Period was a time of experimentation, innovation and compromise. He did everything he could to preserve the real or imagined gains of the revolution while finding new sources of revenue. Fidel never lost his deep dislike of free enterprise and inequality, but gradually allowed more of both, under tight political control. The first major step legalized the possession of US dollars in 1993. Hard cash sent in by relatives in Miami or earned from tourists would be converted into pesos or be spent in state-owned shops that sold essential goods only for dollars. He next allowed 100 categories of self-employment, and co-operative brigades of farmers were permitted to divide up the profits from land and equipment they leased from the state. The following year, he re-established free farmers' markets and, in 1995, private family-owned restaurants. Foreign investments, especially joint ventures with Cuba, were encouraged, though restricted: salaries for Cuban employees, for example, were paid to the state in dollars; the workers got only pesos. Under the new circumstances, some people did better than others. Fidel constantly denounced profiteers and confiscated the money and cars of those who were too successful. Nevertheless, the economy started to show signs of recovery by 1995.

With agriculture, industry and trade at a low ebb, Fidel turned to tourism. This became one of the greatest sources of income, but also potentially the most dangerous and demoralizing. In 1994, 619,000 tourists gave the government a profit of $250 million; five years later over 1.5 million visitors injected some $2 billion into the economy. When the numbers were still small, tourists could be confined to the main resort areas, but they soon started flooding over the whole country. The tourists naturally demanded goods and services. State dollar stores flourished, as did the authorized private restaurants and rooms in private homes, which were taxed heavily. As the state put more goods into the dollar stores, while deliveries to the peso-denominated ration shops became more irregular, people desperately sought dollars. The obvious source was tourists. Doctors abandoned their surgeries to drive taxis, engineers became waiters, and thousands of women turned to prostitution. Cuba was not yet reliving the lascivious days of Batista, when it was justly famed as the whorehouse of the western world, but the sight of Italian gentlemen of a certain age with stunning young Cubans who needed dollars for shoes and dresses became increasingly common. Fidel frequently cracked down: from time to time prostitutes disappeared from the streets of Havana. But they always seemed to come back, for nothing could replace the almighty dollar.

Ideological infection was another danger. Although Cubans had little access to foreign news or papers, tourists could show or tell them what they were missing. The security apparatus and informers could keep some watch on that, but the ubiquitous CDRs were losing their grip as their own members became more involved in the daily struggle. Fortunately for Castro, many of the tourists were young, arriving (especially from Canada) on cheap charter flights.

They loved the country and went home to spread a favourable image that could help sway public opinion. By the end of the decade even Americans were flocking in, most of them in violation of largely unenforced US regulations.

None of this changed the basic structure of the state. Although he emphatically denied being a dictator, Fidel continued to hold all the highest offices and to control everything. What he proposed in a speech on television was soon made into law. He did maintain, though, that every decision was made after consulting the people. In 1990, the *Moscow News* (which was in a position to understand such things) called Cuba a police state. At the end of the decade, the description was still valid. Cosmetic changes did not reduce the monolithic power of the state. In 1993, for example, the National Assembly, which chose the higher bodies of government, was elected by secret ballot for the first time. The results were not surprising: 97 per cent voted for the candidates selected by government-controlled organizations. Fidel himself was also returned, from a district in the Sierra Maestra. His campaign stressed the old values of the revolution. Marx was inevitably yielding to Martí, though the ruling party remained communist.

In 1998, when 98 per cent voted, the candidates were chosen equally by government organizations and local meetings. It hardly mattered, for the Assembly sat only for a few days a year to approve what was put before it.

As Fidel opened up to foreign countries, he came under increasing pressure to relax repression. Danielle Mitterrand, wife of the French president, for example, persuaded him to release six political prisoners in 1995, but no one knew how many others languished in Fidel's camps. Although he told a CNN reporter that he didn't allow an opposition party because the country needed unity above all, he did permit the formation of the Concilio Cubano, a dissident organization that could hope to become a party. In February 1996, though, before it could hold its first meeting, 150 of its leaders were arrested. That was the end of open opposition.

Cuba celebrated the fortieth anniversary of the revolution in January 1999 in a familiar manner, listening to Fidel's speech, broadcast from Santiago. He reminisced about the glorious days of the Sierra, then turned to globalization and the forthcoming collapse of capitalism. A few days later, in a four-and-a-half-hour speech to the national police, he denounced cheating and corruption, and imposed severe new penalties on housebreakers, pimps and drug dealers. These were familiar denunciations and solutions; nothing had changed. Fidel maintained his control over a people whose discontent could never openly be expressed.

For many visitors, the Cuba of the 1990s seemed to be in a time warp. Antique American cars from Batista's days cruised along largely empty streets. The urban fabric of Havana and other cities was intact though crowded and dilapidated. The sight of a building that had crumbled on to the street or was precariously held up by beams was not unusual. On the other hand, the cities were not disfigured by freeways, parking lots, fast food stores or shopping malls, though increasing prosperity at the end of the decade gradually began to change that. Yet tourists rarely saw the vast rings of functional housing that the revolution had built around the cities, or the thousands of new schools, or had occasion to visit the doctors who could be found in any neighbourhood. Despite everything, Castro had managed to preserve the revolution and keep the country going. For the first time in its history, Cuba was truly independent. The price had been high, but for those who still believed in the revolution, it might have seemed justified. The rest could only wait.

NOTES

CHAPTER ONE

1. Szulc, 134.

CHAPTER THREE

1. Fidel Castro, *History Will Absolve Me* (New York: Lyle Stuart, 1961), 79 (many other translations and editions).

CHAPTER FOUR

1. Szulc (paperback edn), 423.
2. Ernesto Che Guevara, *Escritos y discursos* 4 (Havana: Editorial de Ciencias Sociales, 1977), 12.
3. *National Review*, 7 May 1960, 289.
4. Letter to Celia Sánchez, quoted by Franqui, 247.

CHAPTER FIVE

1. Szulc, 485.
2. Quoted by Szulc (paperback edn), 538.

CHAPTER SIX

1. *Life* magazine, 12 April 1963.
2. Quoted by Richard Mahoney, *Sons and Brothers* (New York: Arcade, 1999), 264.
3. Quoted by Quirk, 395.
4. Quoted by Wendy Gimbel, *Havana Dreams* (New York: Vintage, 1998), 143.

CHAPTER SEVEN

1. Quoted by Quirk, 824.

BIBLIOGRAPHY

The most detailed (900-page) biography of Fidel Castro, reasonably objective but a less than gripping read, is:

Quirk, Robert E., *Fidel Castro*, New York: Norton, 1993.

The following are also useful:

Balfour, Sebastian, *Castro*, London: Longman, 1995 (short and clear, very favourable).

Betto, Frei, *Fidel and Religion*, New York: Simon & Schuster, 1987 (interview, with many details of his early life).

Bourne, Peter, *Fidel*, New York: Dodd, Mead, 1986 (psychological, colourful).

Castro, Fidel, *History Will Absolve Me*, New York: Lyle Stuart, 1961, and many other editions (speech at trial).

Fidel Castro: Nothing Can Stop the Course of History, interview by Jeffrey M. Elliot and Mervyn M. Dymally, New York: Pathfinder, 1986.

Fernandez, Alina, *Castro's Daughter*, New York: St Martin's, 1998 (outspokenly negative).

Franqui, Carlos, *Family Portrait with Fidel*, New York: Random House, 1984 (negative account by a revolutionary).

Geyer, Georgie Anne, *Guerrilla Prince: The Untold Story of Fidel Castro*, Boston: Little, Brown, 1991 (unfavourable; often unreliable in details).

Bibliography

Guevara, Ernesto Che, *Episodes of the Cuban Revolutionary War*, New York: Pathfinder, 1996 (vivid personal account of the revolution).

Lockwood, Lee, *Castro's Cuba, Cuba's Fidel*, New York: Macmillan, 1967 (interview).

Morejón, Gerardo Rodriguez, *Fidel Castro Biografia*, Havana: Fernandez, 1959 (first biography; hagiographic but with many interesting details and photos).

Oppenheimer, Andres, *Castro's Final Hour*, New York: Simon & Schuster, 1992.

Pérez, Louis, *Cuba between Reform and Revolution,* Oxford University Press, 1988 (general background).

Russo, Gus, *Live by the Sword: The Secret War against Castro and the Death of JFK*, Baltimore: Bancroft, 1998.

La Sierra y el Llano, Havana: Casa de las Americas, 1969 (collection of revolutionary memoirs).

Suchlicki, Jaime, *Cuba from Columbus to Castro*, New York: Brassey's, 1998 (general background).

Szulc, Tad, *Fidel, A Critical Portrait*, New York: Morrow, 1986 (vivid, superb account of the revolution and first years of Castro's rule).

Thomas, Hugh, *Cuba, The Pursuit of Freedom*, New York: Harper & Row, 1971 (monumental history up to 1970).